WILD BROTHERS
OF THE
INDIANS

As pictured by the Ancient Americans

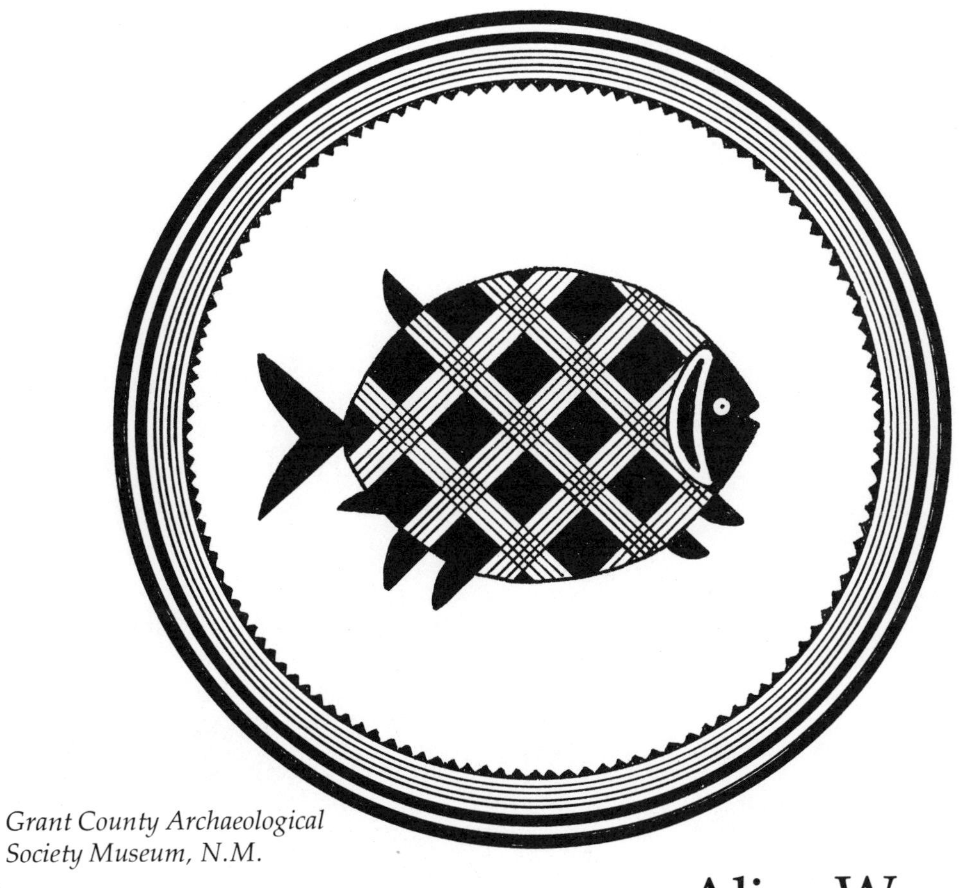

Grant County Archaeological Society Museum, N.M.

Alice Wesche

$4.95

WILD BROTHERS of the INDIANS

ISBN 0-918080-21-5
Library of Congress No. 77-790-64

TREASURE CHEST PUBLICATIONS, INC.
P.O. Box 5250—Tucson, Arizona 85703
Printed in Phoenix, Arizona
by Associated Lithographers

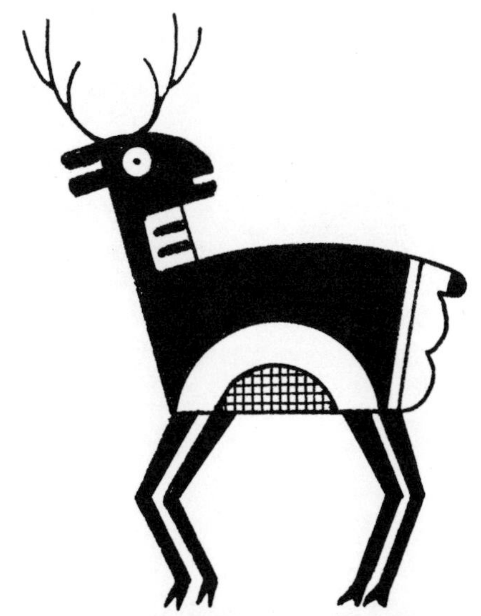

Now comes the deer up to our house.
He brings the needed food of life,
While we give needed food to him.

Spinden, *"Songs of the Tewa"*

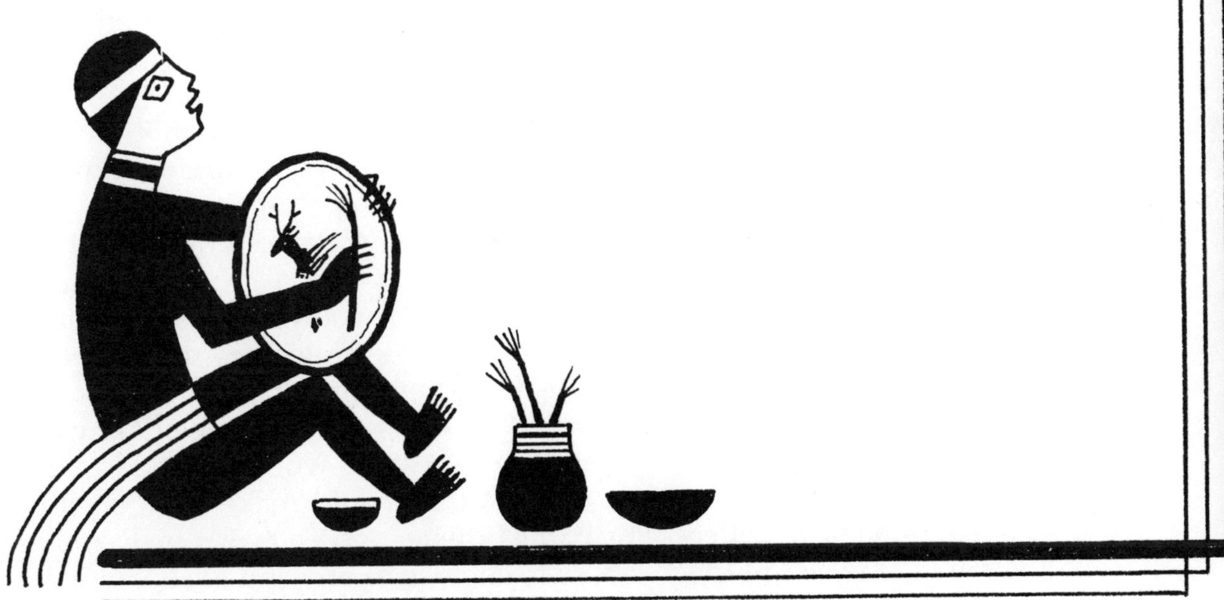

The early Indians expressed their kinship with their Wild Brothers by picturing them in many ways. They used whatever materials Nature provided, and only such simple tools as they could make for themselves. In this book you will see how, using the tools of today, you can draw many of these creatures to look like those drawn by one small tribe of Indians 1000 years ago.

"Very long ago the trees, the animals and birds and fish, also the grass and rocks and mountains and all things in Nature could talk together, including people, who in turn could talk to them. And so all things came to know each other and to understand each other better."

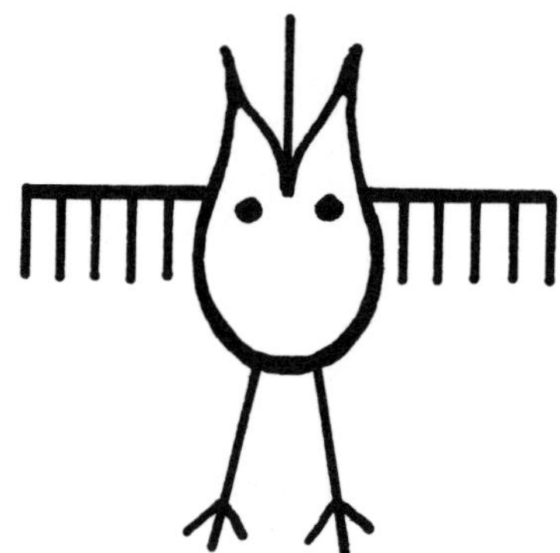

These are the words of a wise old Hopi Indian as he repeats a story his Grandmother had told him, when he was a small boy, about a time when the world was new. Most present day Indian tribes have such legends, told to the children of each generation, of how, in the beginning, people were much closer to the other animals, and all tried to live together in harmony.

Certainly we know that before white men came to this land the earlier peoples of the forests and deserts, the plains and mountains and seashores, liked to make pictures of the wild creatures that shared their lands. Some carved them on rocks, or engraved them on shells or bones. Some painted them on the clay pots they made, or cave walls. Some fashioned them in wood, or wove them in baskets or blankets. Always, it seems, the things they most liked to picture were the Wild Brothers they knew so well.

These early people learned to use whatever materials were most plentiful, whether stone or clay or wood or reeds, and worked with such simple tools as they could make from shell or rocks or deer antlers. For paint brushes, green twigs or the long slender leaves of the yucca were chewed at one end to separate the fibers, thus forming bristles. Paints were made from finely powdered clays containing minerals that gave them a red or yellow or tan color when mixed with water. White paint was made from a white earth called kaolin, while black could be made from boiled plant juices sometimes mixed with charcoal and ground minerals. Colors for woven baskets and blankets were made from berries, and from wild plants such as the flowers and bark of rabbitbrush. Dyes were also made from minerals dug from the ground.

It must have taken long years of patiently trying many ways of working with such simple tools and materials to produce the many things these people made. And all the ways they learned they taught to their children, who then went on to make even better carvings and paintings, always staying close to Mother Earth and all her living things.

As we look at the wild creatures pictured by the Indians, it seems they must have thought of them as familiar friends and neighbors. They also believed that divine beings often appeared on earth in animal forms, or used certain creatures as their messengers to men. Today, among the older Navajo and Pueblo Indians there are still those who believe that a man who lives right and thinks good thoughts can, if he wishes, change himself into the animal that is his Clan Brother, be it fox or serpent or other creature.

Some of the Pueblos of the Rio Grande Valley still have ceremonial dances in which the dancers are dressed to resemble deer or mountain sheep or eagles, and as they dance they imitate the motions of these animals.

Deer dancers wear evergreen, the symbol of long life.

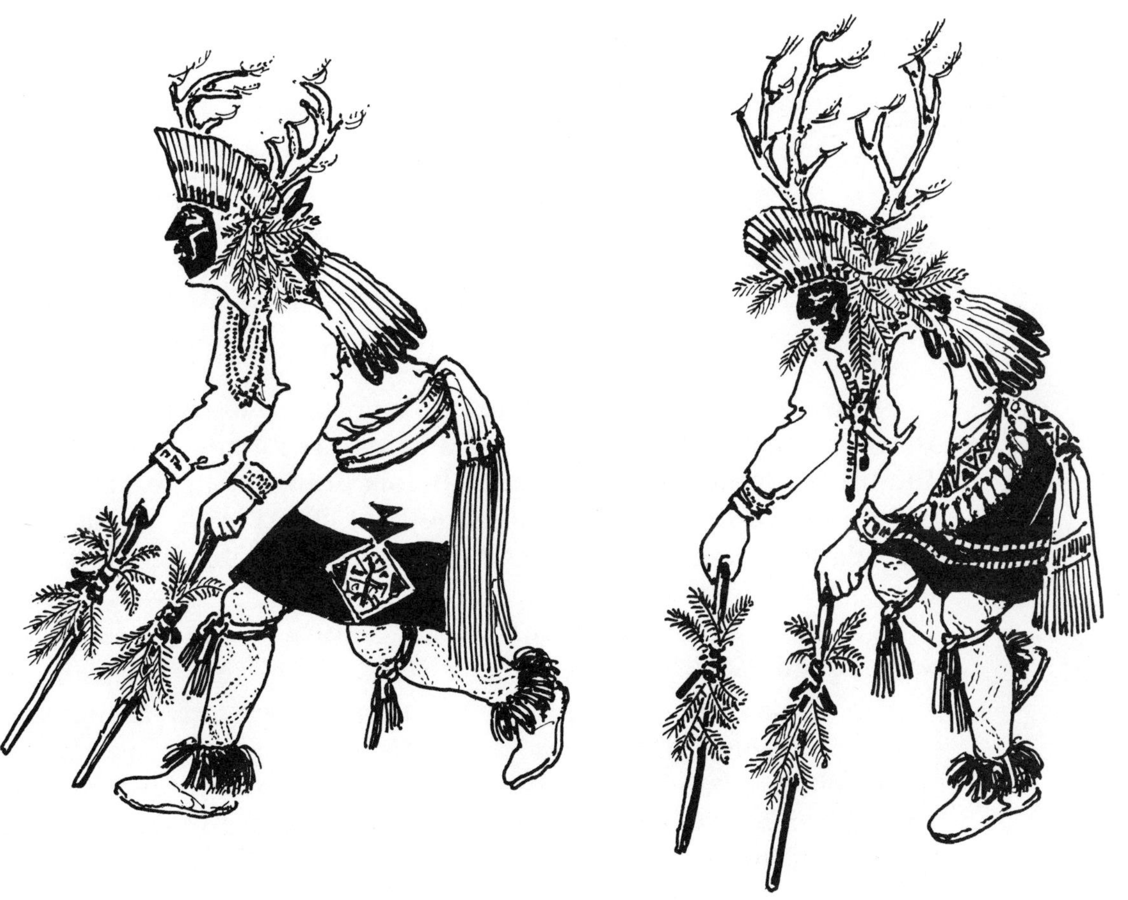

It was, of course, necessary for early Indian people to kill animals of all sorts, even crickets, in order to eat and so stay alive. But we know of no tribe that killed for sport as some white men do today. Always before a hunt, offerings had to be made and prayers said, asking permission for the kill. There are many stories of people who were severely punished for purposely crushing a beetle, or stepping on a snake for no good reason.

Southward, in what is now Mexico, the calendar was divided into groups of twenty days each instead of the seven days we have in each week. The people had no written language so they used pictures to represent the names of the days. Exactly half of these were drawings of animals or birds.

The Day of the

Serpent... *Crocodile...* *Lizard...* *Vulture...* *Dog...*

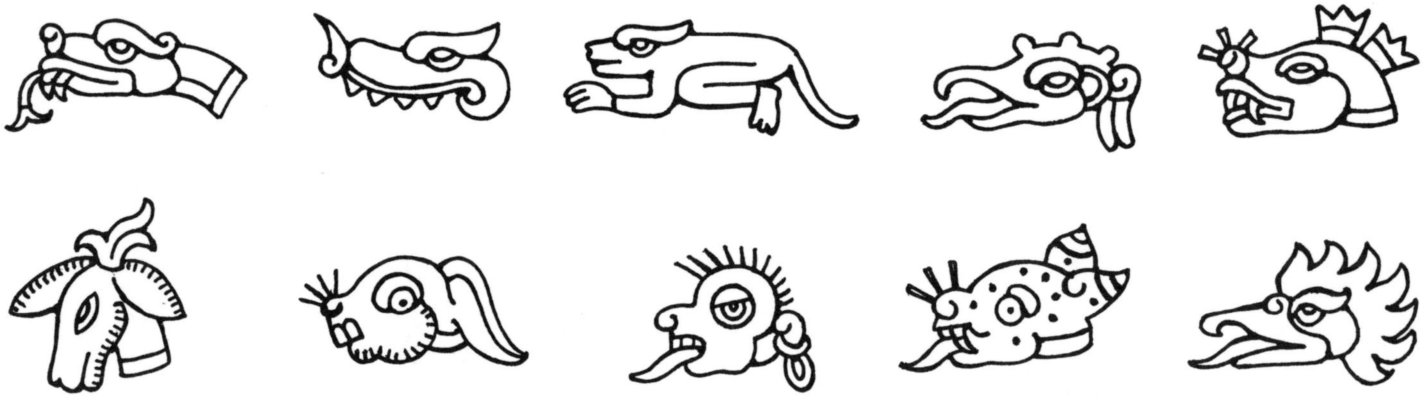

Deer... *Rabbit...* *Monkey...* *Jaguar...* *Eagle...*

Farther north, in New Mexico, the Zuni children were taught that long ago, while yet all living things belonged to one family, they were protected on all sides by six animals. In the North the Mountain Lion stood guard, in the East stood Wolf, in the South was Badger, in the West was Bear. Above, Eagle shielded them, and below Mole kept watch. In many Museums you may still see little carved stone figures, or fetishes, of these "Prey Gods" as they were called.

Not all Indians everywhere pictured the same animals. I'm sure you would not expect people living in desert lands to draw pictures of whales, or those in the far north to draw monkeys. Also, the materials they found to work with had much to do with how they painted their Wild Brothers.

For example, the many tribes living along the Nothwest Coast from Alaska to Oregon got much of their food from the ocean, and traveled on the water from village to village. So they knew well the sea creatures,—whales and fish and seals. On land they found bears and beaver and wolves, with eagles overhead. Great forests of red cedar grew almost to the water's edge, so wood was plentiful, as were shell and bone and stone. So the people of these tribes with the strange names, (Nootka, Tlingit, Kwakiutl), carved the cedar into roofposts and large screens to divide the houses into rooms. They also carved and painted boxes and chests and dishes, and strange masks to wear in ceremonies, and even long seagoing canoes holding many men. All these things were decorated with carvings of the animals they knew best. Often they used bits of pretty shell for eyes or teeth of the animals. The women wove robes of wild goat hair and shredded cedar bark, and on these, too, animals were shown.

All of this work was done with stone tools they made for themselves. Years later, when white men brought steel axes and knives to the West, these Indians carved whole trees into tall "totem poles" which they set up in front of the villages facing the sea. But before they had steel they carved only the shorter poles needed for their houses.

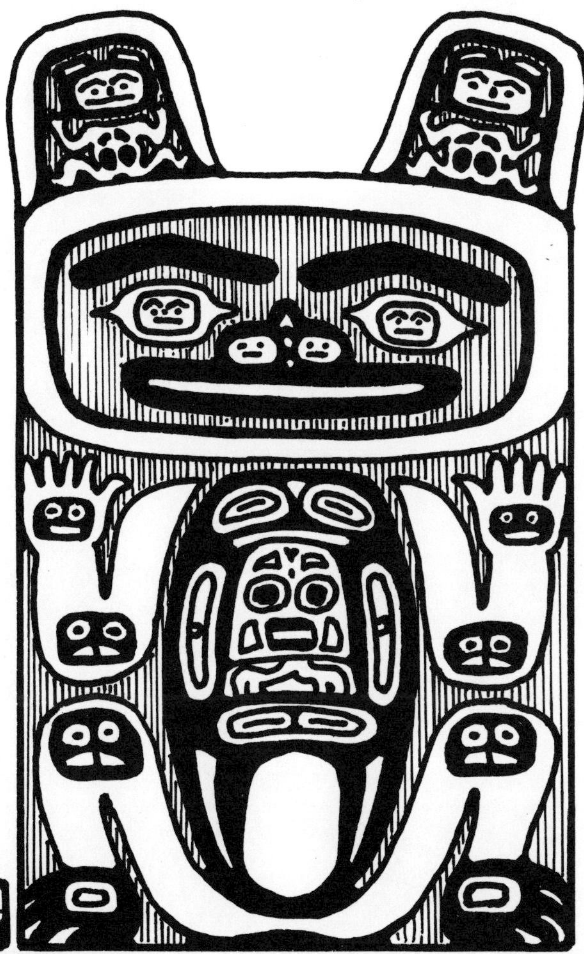

This carved and painted bear was part of a house wall.

In the dry lands of our American Southwest the early Indians lived a quite different kind of life. Here wood was scarce and often had to be carried long distances from the hills where it grew to villages in the small river valleys. But there was plenty of good clay for making pottery, also the white earth used to coat the pots to give them a fine surface for painting, and the minerals for black, red, and yellow paints. So it is not surprising that most of the animal art of the Pueblo people and other desert dwellers was painted on clay bowls and jars. These people also pictured the eagle and bear, but more often they painted deer, rabbits, lizards, and many kinds of birds and insects.

Birds and butterflies were painted on jars.

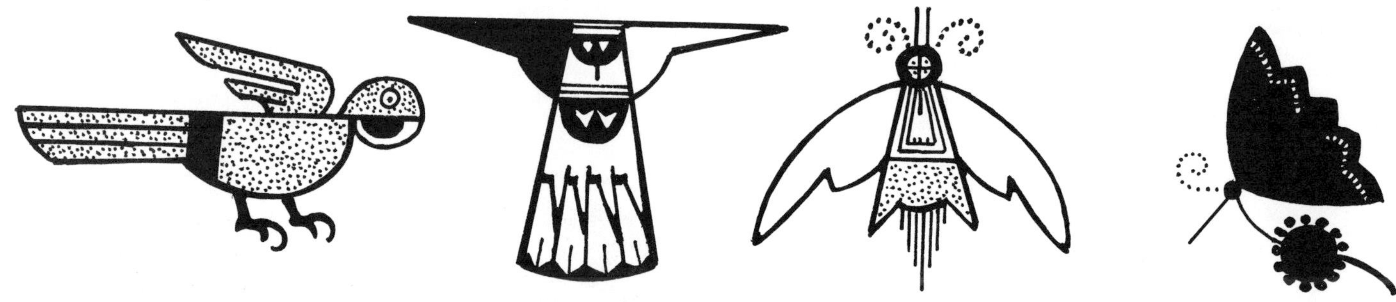

This was a rocky country, with deep canyons and many caves. On the cave walls and the rocks the villagers and wandering hunters pictured the animals of their land, either with paint or by pecking the rock with tools of harder stone. Thus they showed wolves, snakes, deer and many other creatures. These were not as well drawn as those on the bowls, for of course it was much harder work.

Early rock carvings are found in many places in the southwestern states.

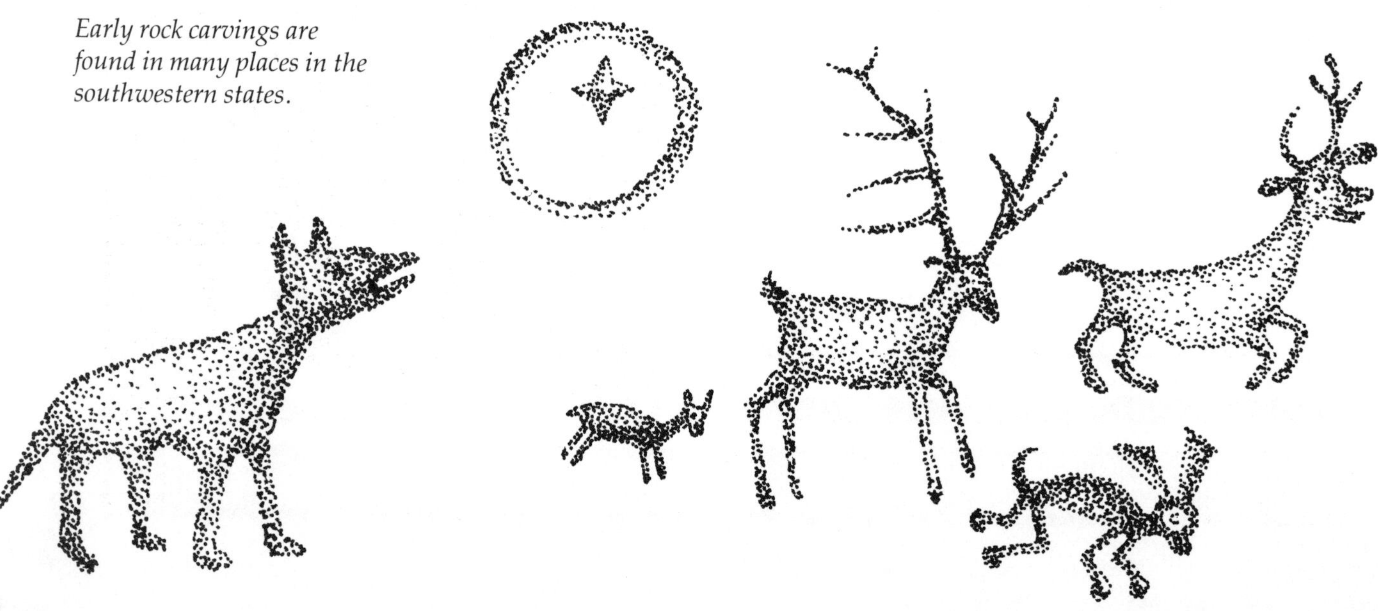

Eastward from the desert country lies rolling grassland with many large rivers and lakes and woods. In this wide and pleasant land were many Indian tribes with different ideas and beliefs and ways of living, but with the same brotherly feeling for the wild creatures as the Indians of the North and the West. So they, too, made animal pictures, which were found hundreds of years later by the white men—pictures carved in stone, shaped in clay, scratched on shells, or whittled in wood.

One material they had which was not much used by the desert folk. This was copper, which they dug from the ground and hammered flat, then shaped like birds or other creatures.

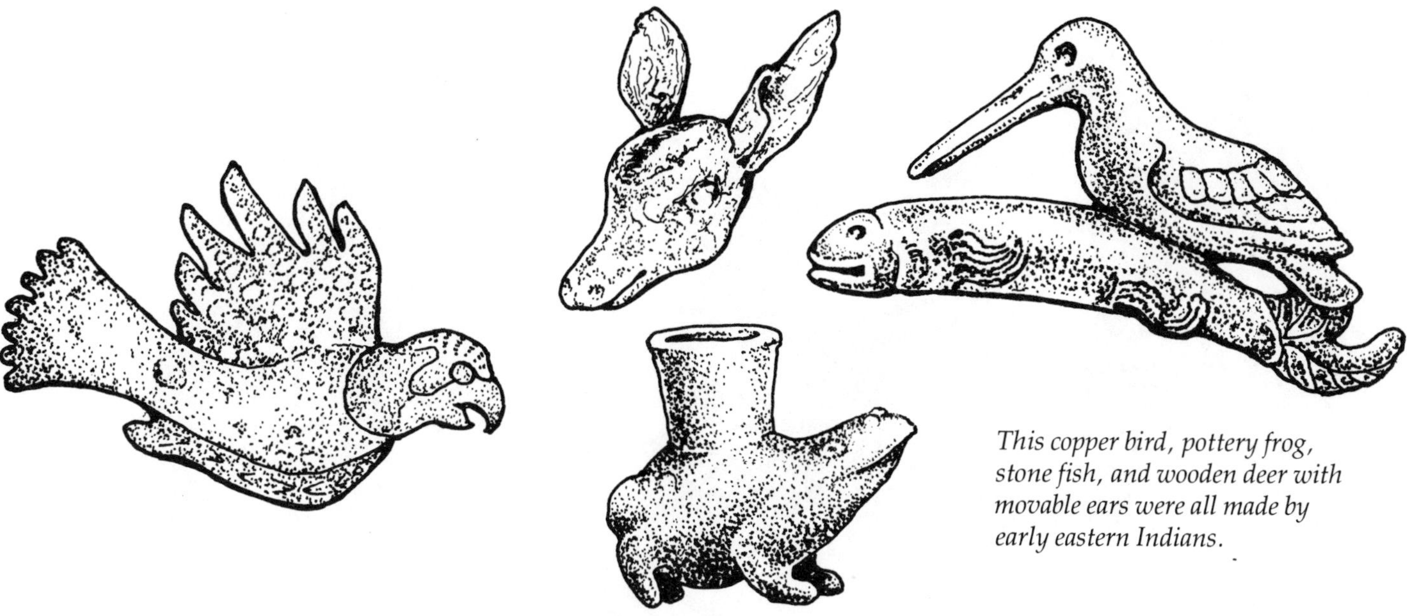

This copper bird, pottery frog, stone fish, and wooden deer with movable ears were all made by early eastern Indians.

But the largest animal picture they made and left for us to see and wonder at is one fourth of a mile long—a great snake formed of earth heaped up in a long curvey mound almost as high as a man!

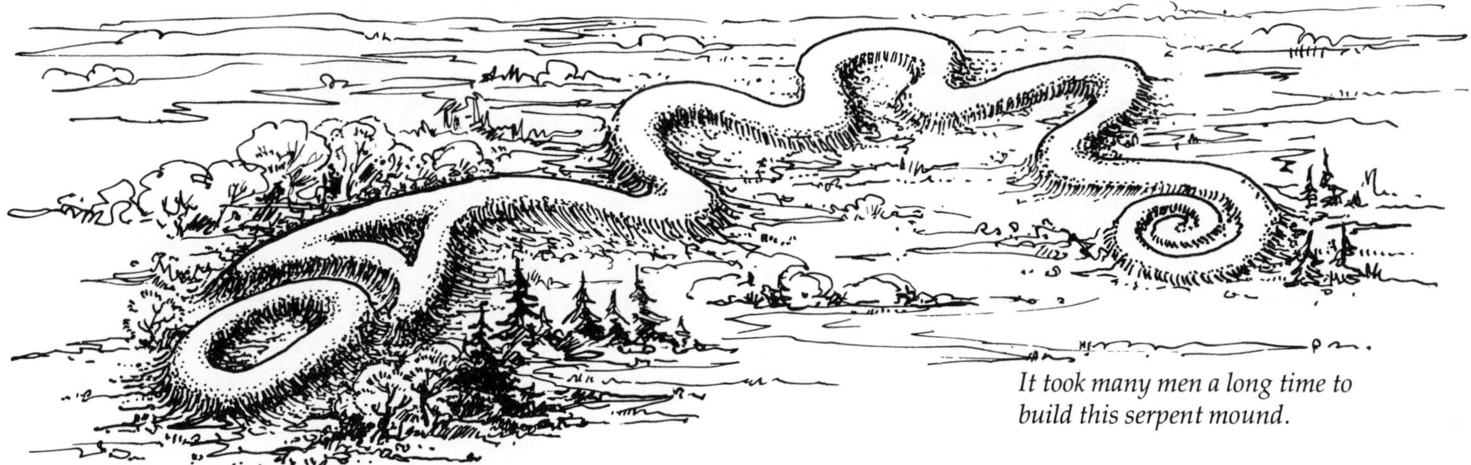

It took many men a long time to build this serpent mound.

Far to the south lived Indians of another kind, with other beliefs and ideas, and many other animals. These people built large cities, with tall temples of stone carved and painted outside and inside. Like their northern neighbors, they made pottery, wove clothing, carved wood and shell and stone. But they had still another way of picturing the animals they knew best. They made folding books of soft skins, and, as they had no written language, they told the stories in these books with pictures. Among these pictures are many drawings of the birds and beasts and reptiles of that land, beautifully painted in many colors.

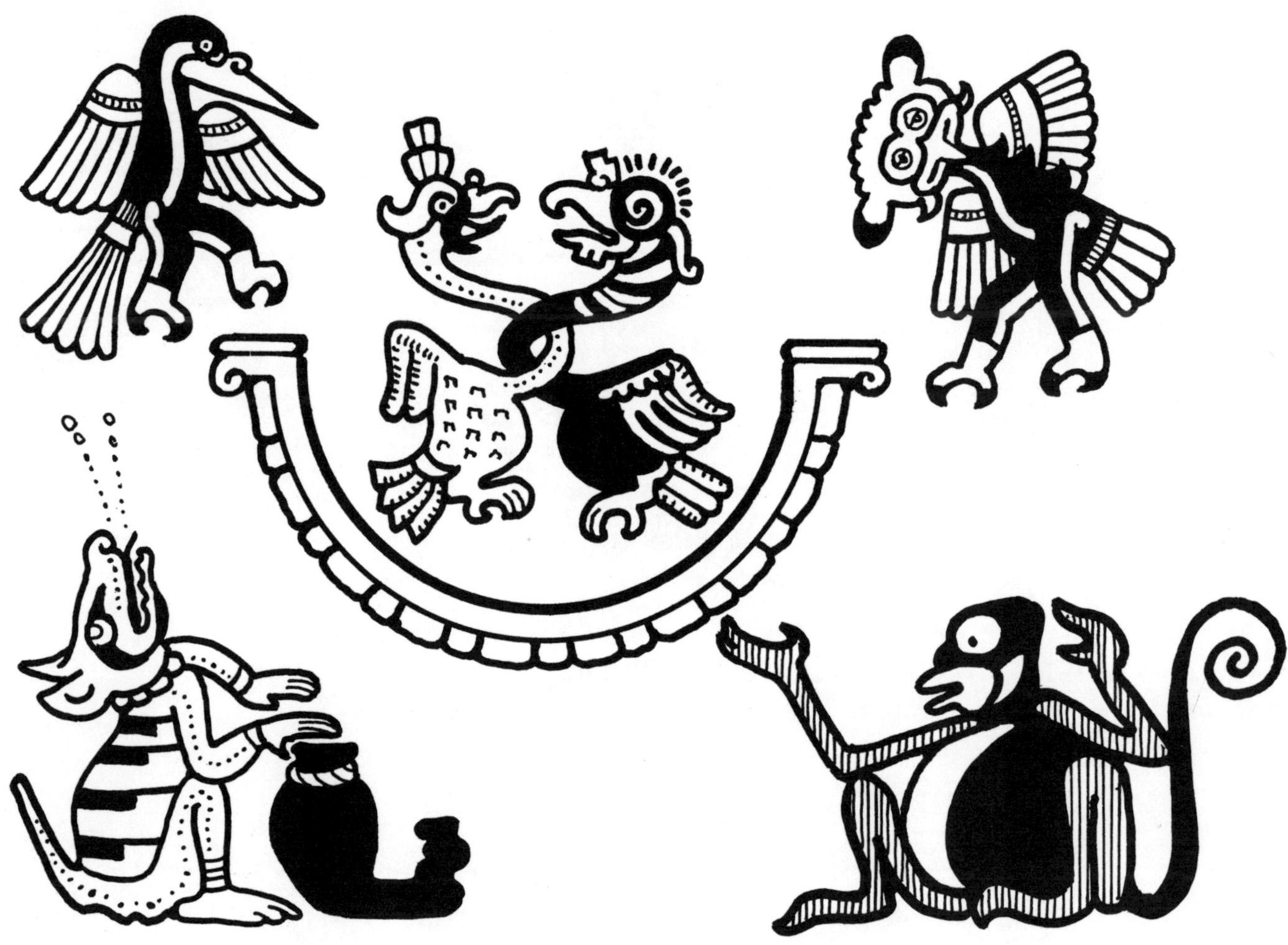

These creatures were painted on pages of animal skin.

These Indians of the South also gathered the feathers of many bright colored birds, and with these they wove robes and shields decorated with animal pictures, sometimes outlining them with gold.

Along the mountainous west coast of South America there long ago lived Indians who were very clever at working with the gold and silver which they dug from the hills. This they melted and poured into molds, or hammered into sheets which they formed into beautiful jewelry. From the silver they also made small figures of the longlegged animals that lived in the hills,—the llama, vicuna, and alpaca, which looked rather like humpless camels.

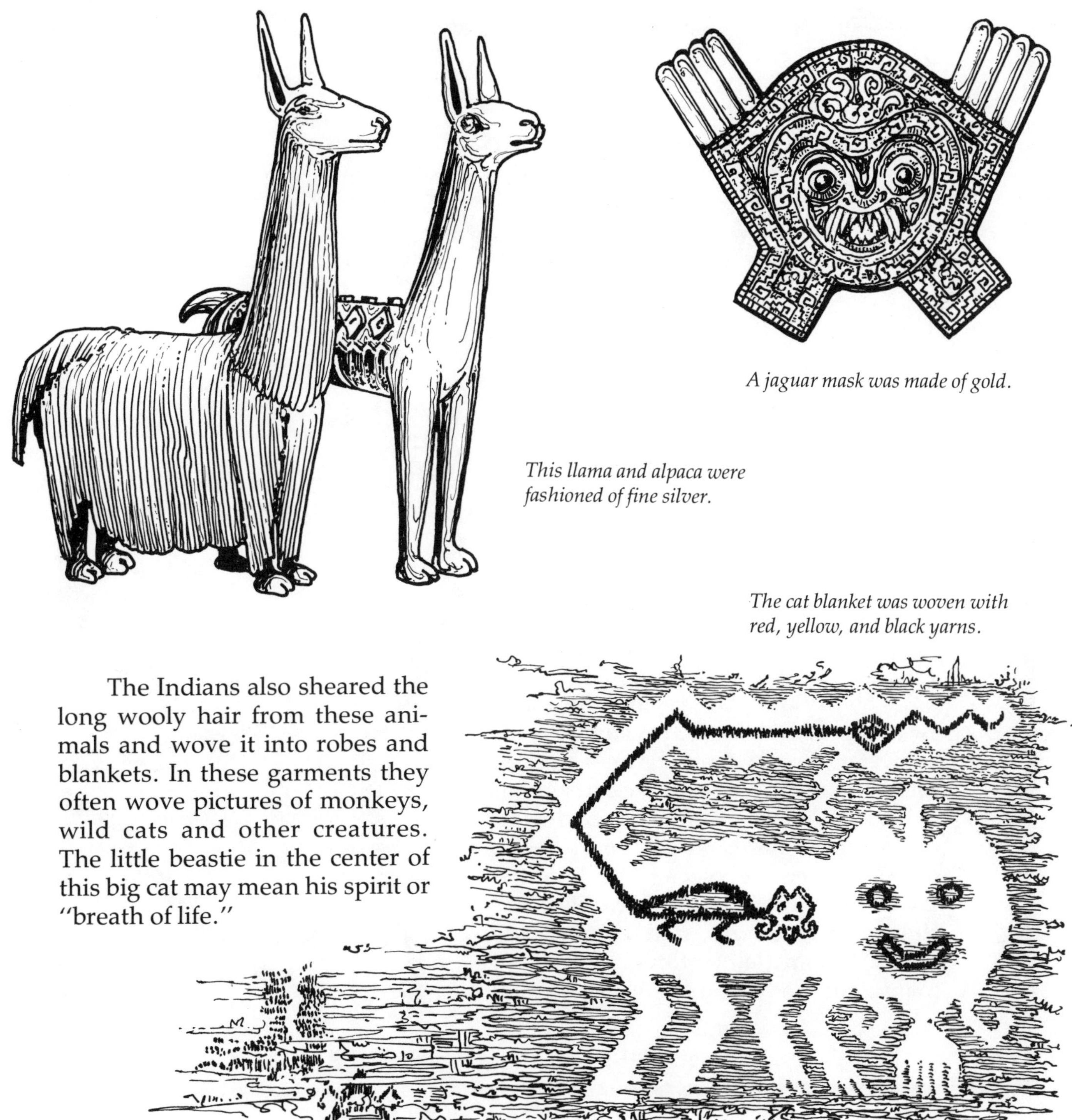

A jaguar mask was made of gold.

This llama and alpaca were fashioned of fine silver.

The cat blanket was woven with red, yellow, and black yarns.

The Indians also sheared the long wooly hair from these animals and wove it into robes and blankets. In these garments they often wove pictures of monkeys, wild cats and other creatures. The little beastie in the center of this big cat may mean his spirit or "breath of life."

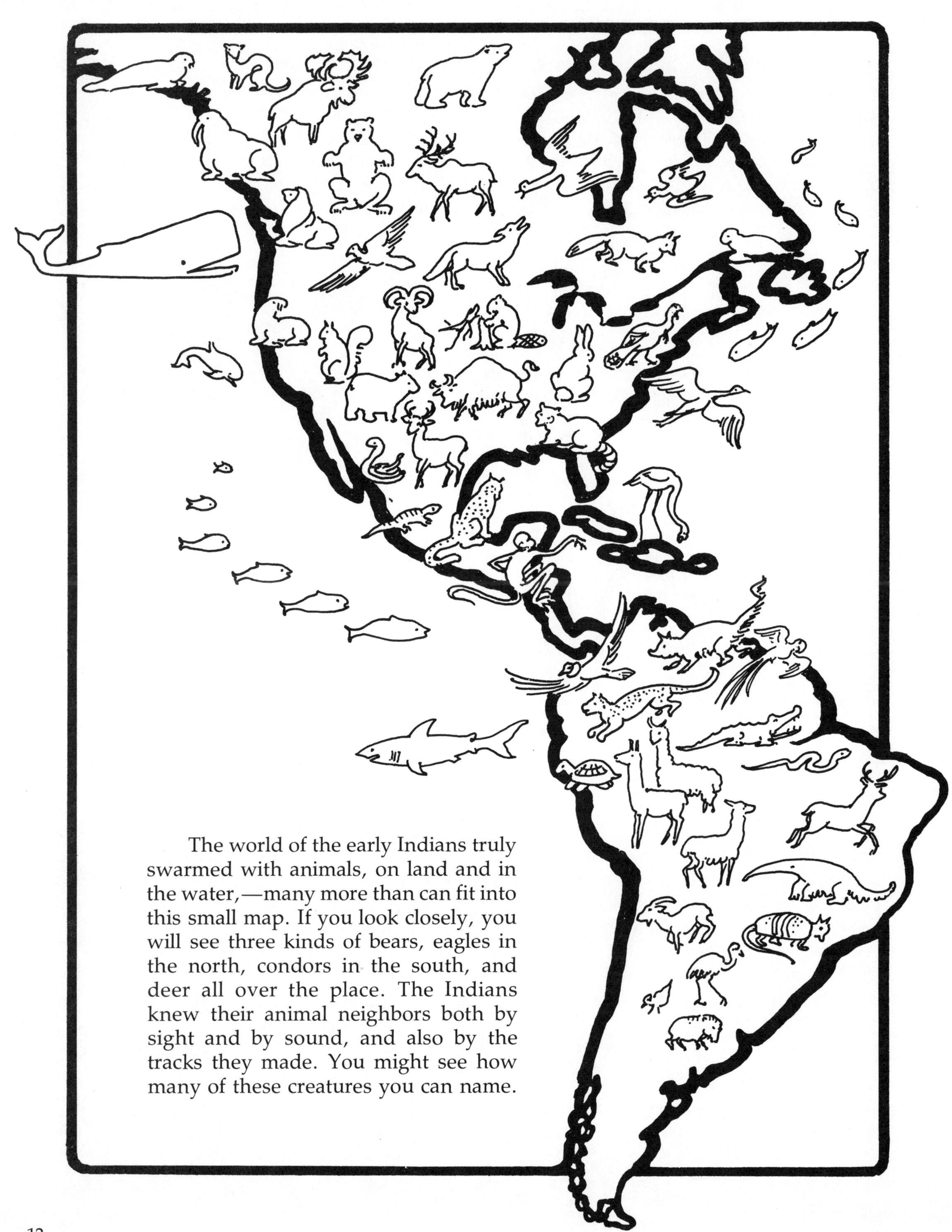

The world of the early Indians truly swarmed with animals, on land and in the water,—many more than can fit into this small map. If you look closely, you will see three kinds of bears, eagles in the north, condors in the south, and deer all over the place. The Indians knew their animal neighbors both by sight and by sound, and also by the tracks they made. You might see how many of these creatures you can name.

Indians of all times and places seem to have had an especially friendly feeling for the deer family. About 1000 years ago an Indian living in the Grand Canyon of Colorado made this deer of split twigs lashed together with strips of bark, and left it in his cave hidden high up in the Canyon wall.

Far to the south and many centuries later, the Indians of Mexico were drawing books of pictures, as they had no written language. This is how they wrote the word "deer."

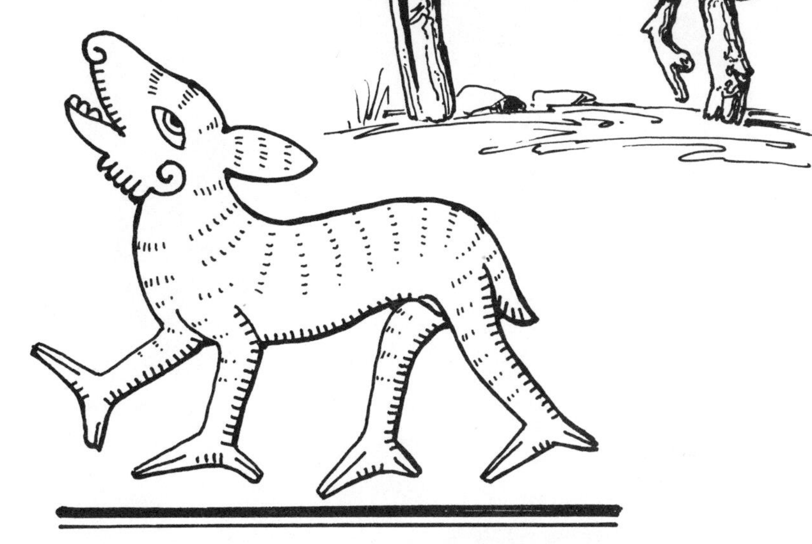

Still farther south, the Indians of the Andes Highlands shaped this clay figure of a mother deer clasping her two little fawns in her arms.

Now that you have seen some of the many ways the early people of the Americas pictured the wild creatures that shared their lands, we will look at one small tribe that, during the short span of about 300 years, painted thousands of the most charming animal pictures ever made.

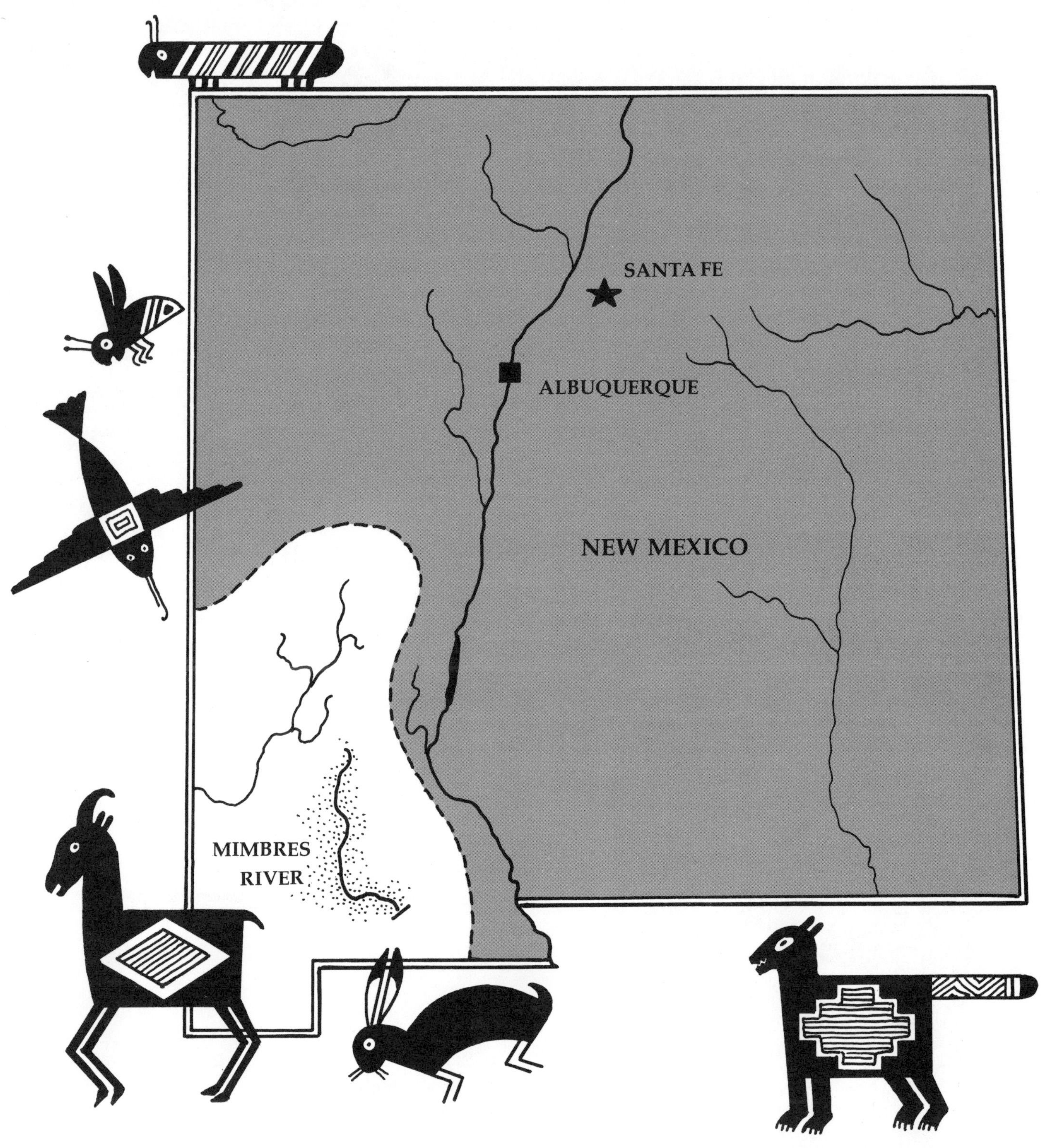

As you look at the map of New Mexico you will see, down in the southwest corner, a small river that seems to go nowhere—not to an ocean, or to a lake, or to another river. It just flows southward and disappears. This is the Mimbres River, and here in this Valley about a thousand years ago a quite surprising thing happened.

In that far-off time the River was wider and deeper, and probably flowed onward to empty into a lake instead of going underground. The people who lived in the valley were glad to have the River to water their small fields of corn and beans. They were a peaceful people, whose grandfathers had come to this place many years before and had built their villages on the low ridges bordering the River. They gathered food from wild plants as well as from their fields, while the men brought in meat, for game was plentiful. Like most people in early days, they made cooking pots of clay, at first quite simple ones. As the potters became more skillful they decorated their work by scratching lines in the wet clay, or by pinching it into designs with their fingers. They also learned to coat the vessels with a thin layer of white clay and to then draw patterns on it with black paint.

Then, about the year 900, some innovative potter began to decorate the insides of the white bowls with drawings of the animals that shared the valley homeland. This was a really new idea, and the other villagers in the surrounding country must have liked it, for soon hundreds of bowls were being painted with pictures of rabbits, mountain goats, fish, birds, and even people. These primitive folk must have had a close and friendly understanding of their wild brothers, and very observant eyes, for as you look at the following pages you will see how skillful they were in drawing each creature in its own special form and character. While each picture of a rabbit, for example, is different from all the others, still all look unmistakably like rabbits.

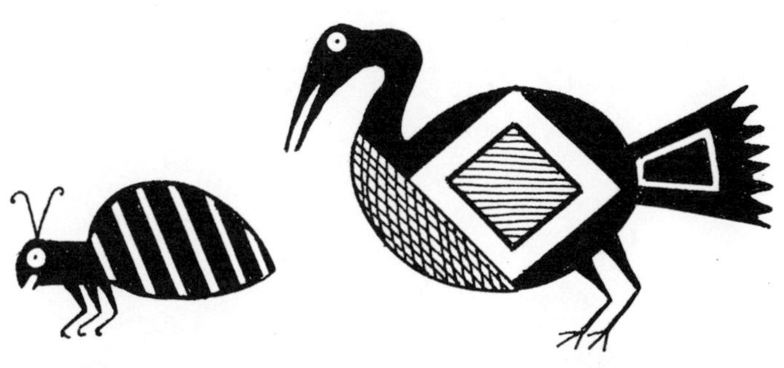

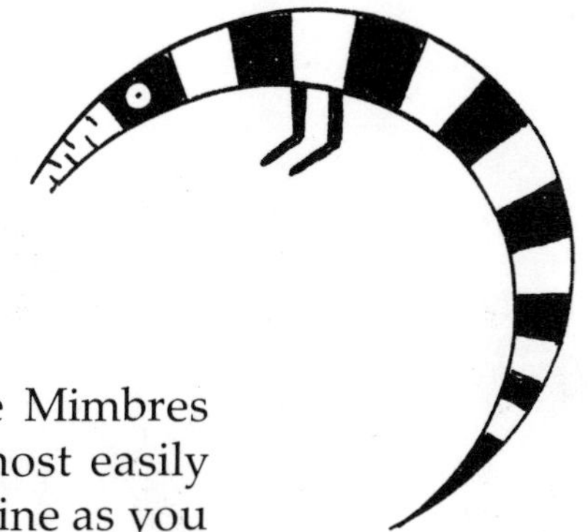

Opposite each page of animals, drawn just as the Mimbres potters drew them, is a page showing how you can most easily draw these animals. Draw lightly until you have the outline as you want it, then add decoration in lines or solids using designs shown or making others of your own. But first we will see how the potters made the bowls in which they painted these animals.

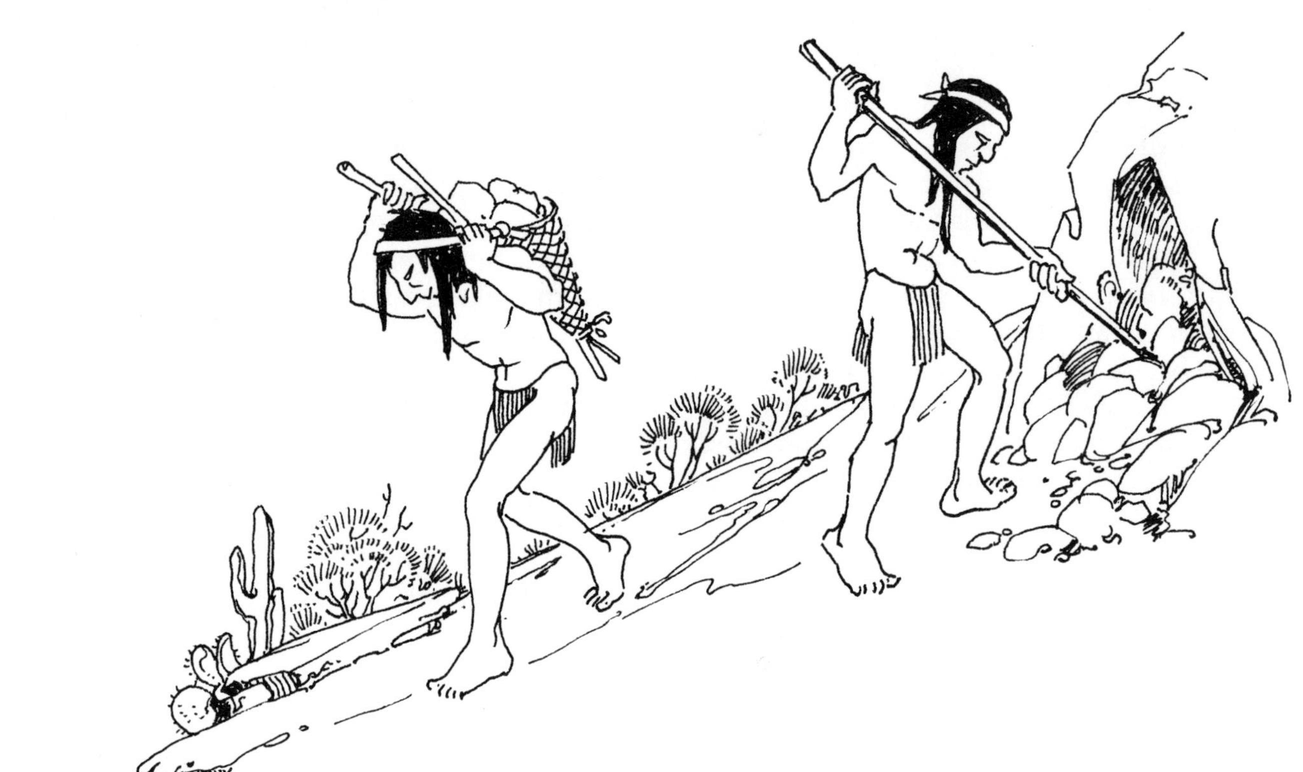

Good clay for making pottery could be found in many places along the Mimbres Valley. It was dug with wooden digging sticks and carried to the village in baskets or in bags made of skins. In the village the women went to work on it, beating and crushing it into fine powder. Then it was sifted through a gourd with fine holes in it, removing lumps and bits of stone. Next it was mixed with water and a little fine sand to keep it from cracking, and kneaded like bread dough till smooth. Ropes of this dough were made by rolling it between the hands. A lump of the dough was put in a shallow basket or the bottom of a broken pot which had been sprinkled with fine wood ash to keep the clay from sticking. The clay was then pulled and pinched up around the rim, and a coil of clay rope laid along the edge and smoothed in. Enough coils were added to make the bowl as big as the potter wished.

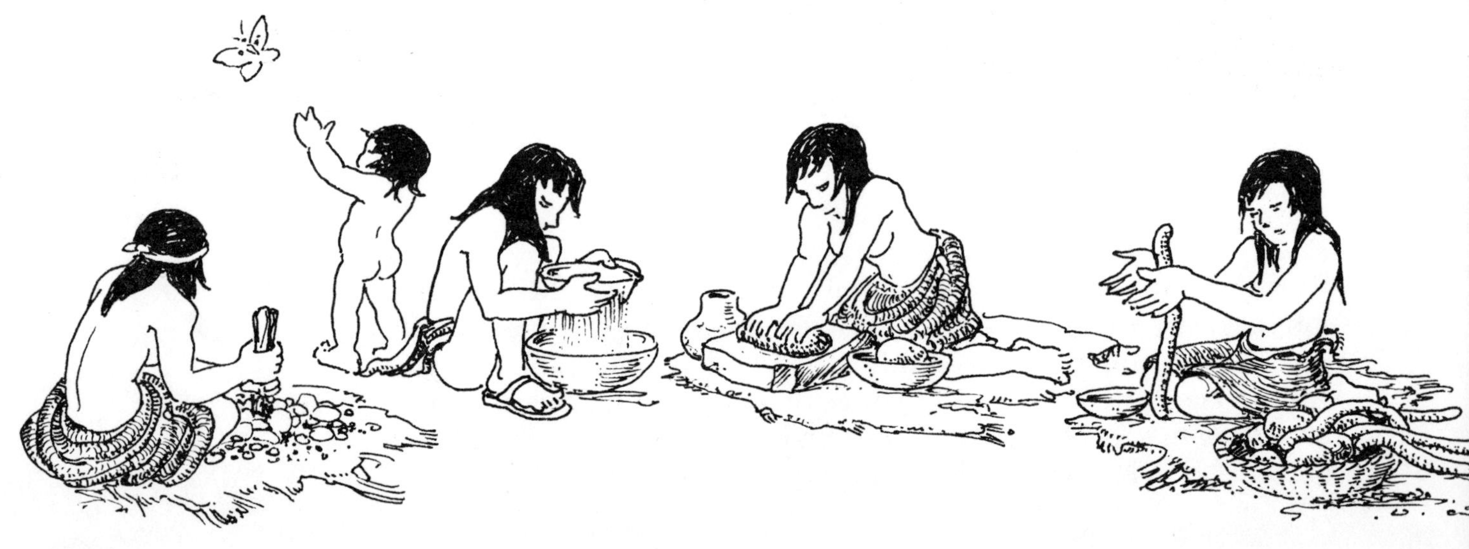

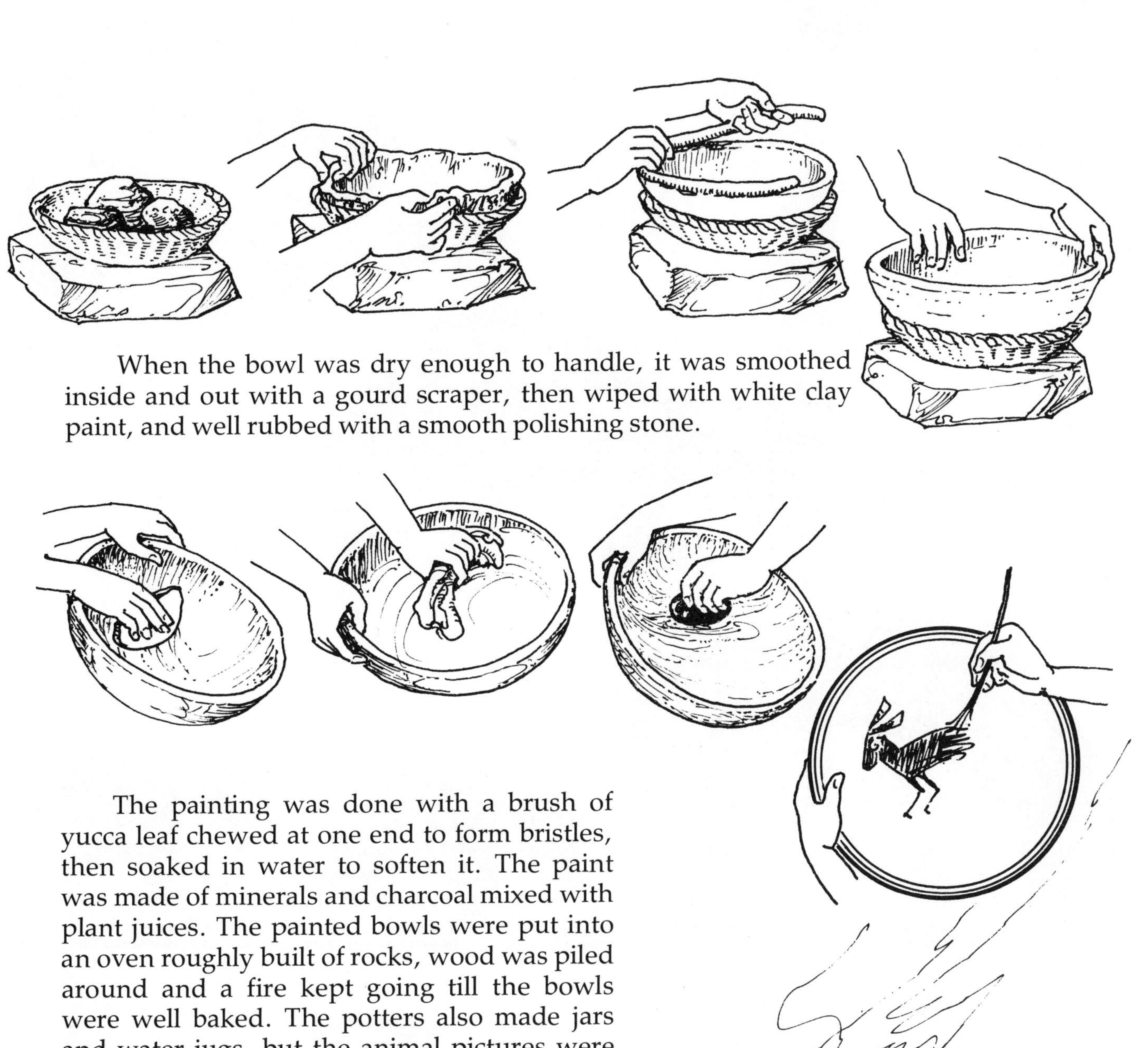

When the bowl was dry enough to handle, it was smoothed inside and out with a gourd scraper, then wiped with white clay paint, and well rubbed with a smooth polishing stone.

The painting was done with a brush of yucca leaf chewed at one end to form bristles, then soaked in water to soften it. The paint was made of minerals and charcoal mixed with plant juices. The painted bowls were put into an oven roughly built of rocks, wood was piled around and a fire kept going till the bowls were well baked. The potters also made jars and water jugs, but the animal pictures were made on the bowls.

Now are you ready to begin drawing your own family of wild Brothers? . . . . . .

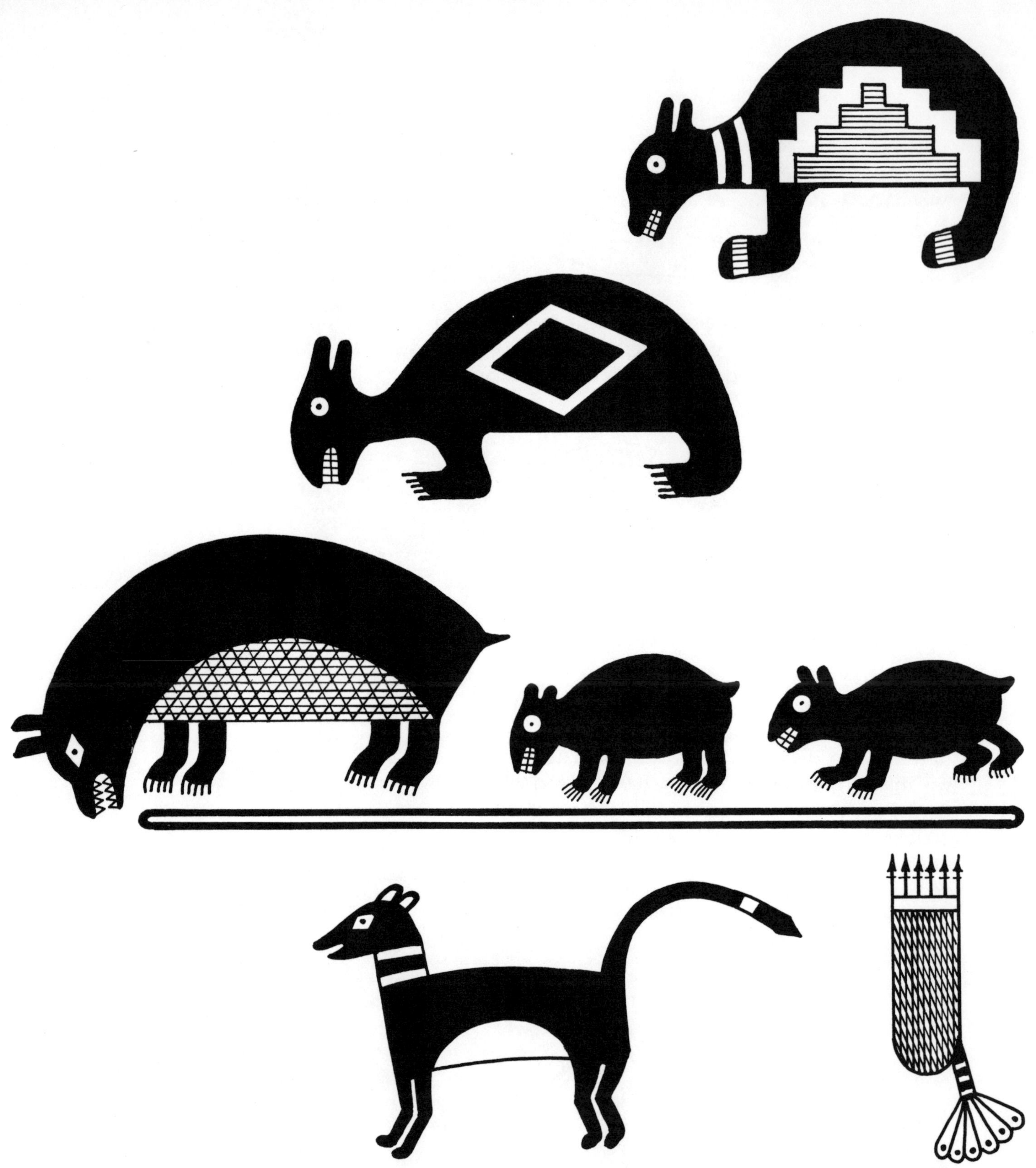

Black bears lived in the high forests. When guarding her young cubs the mother bear could be very dangerous. Notice the teeth on these animals, and the strong claws on the short legs. When going to the forest the hunter would take his dog and his quiver of arrows which you see lower on the page.

Mimbres bears fit well into circles. Draw your circle lightly so you can erase the part you don't use.

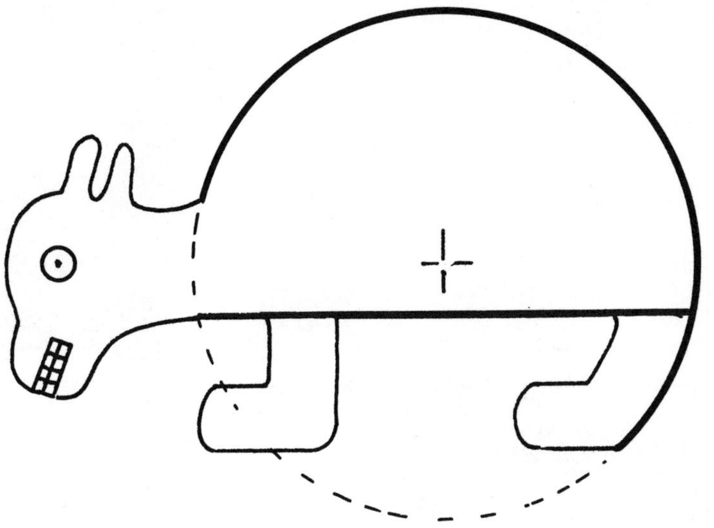

This bear uses a little more than a half circle. Notice the small cross which marks the circle center, and draw the long line just below it. Then add the head and thick legs, not forgetting claws and teeth.

The next bear uses a bit less than half the circle. Bears have very short tails which do not show at all on these first two bears.

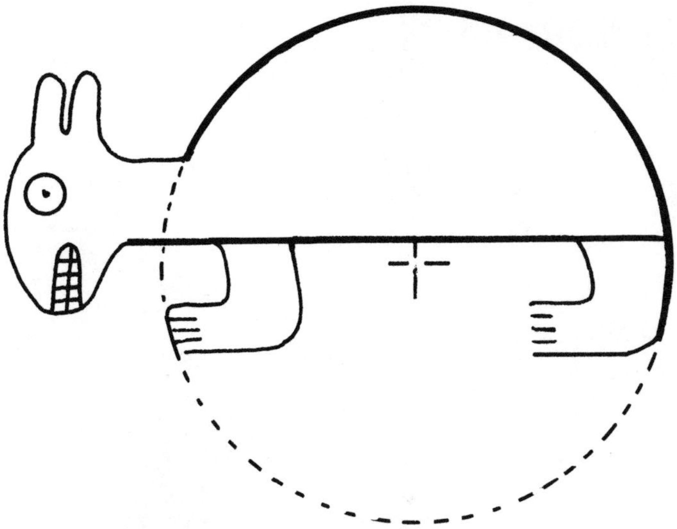

The third bear is drawn with circle-in-a-circle. He seems to be standing on a cliff edge, looking over. You might draw a pattern of some sort on his under side.

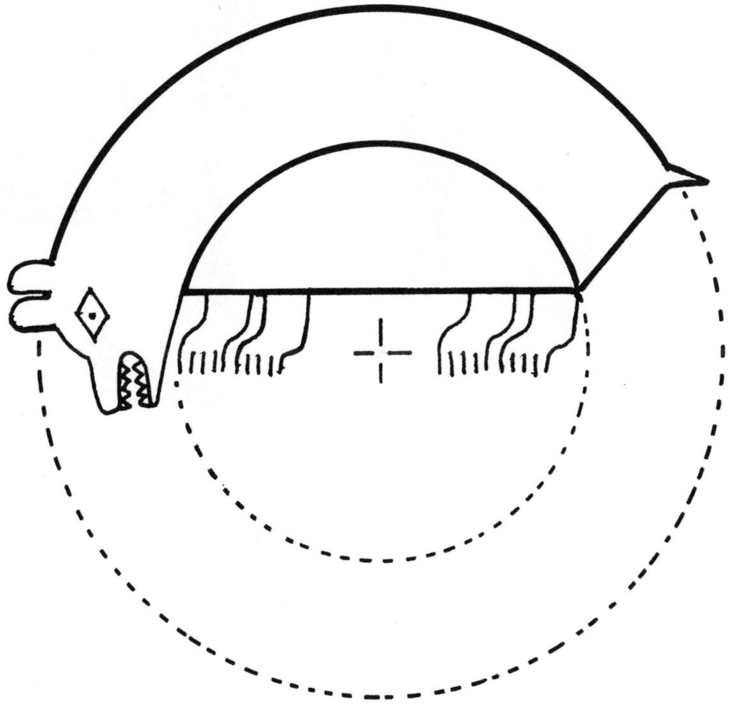

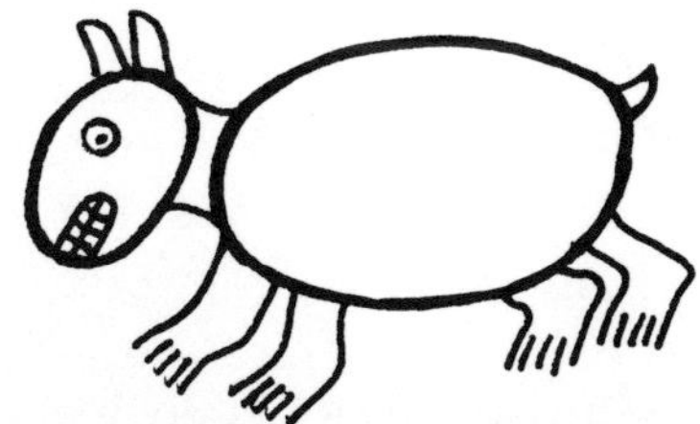

This little cub is formed from two ovals, with added legs and tail. Young though he is he already has sharp teeth.

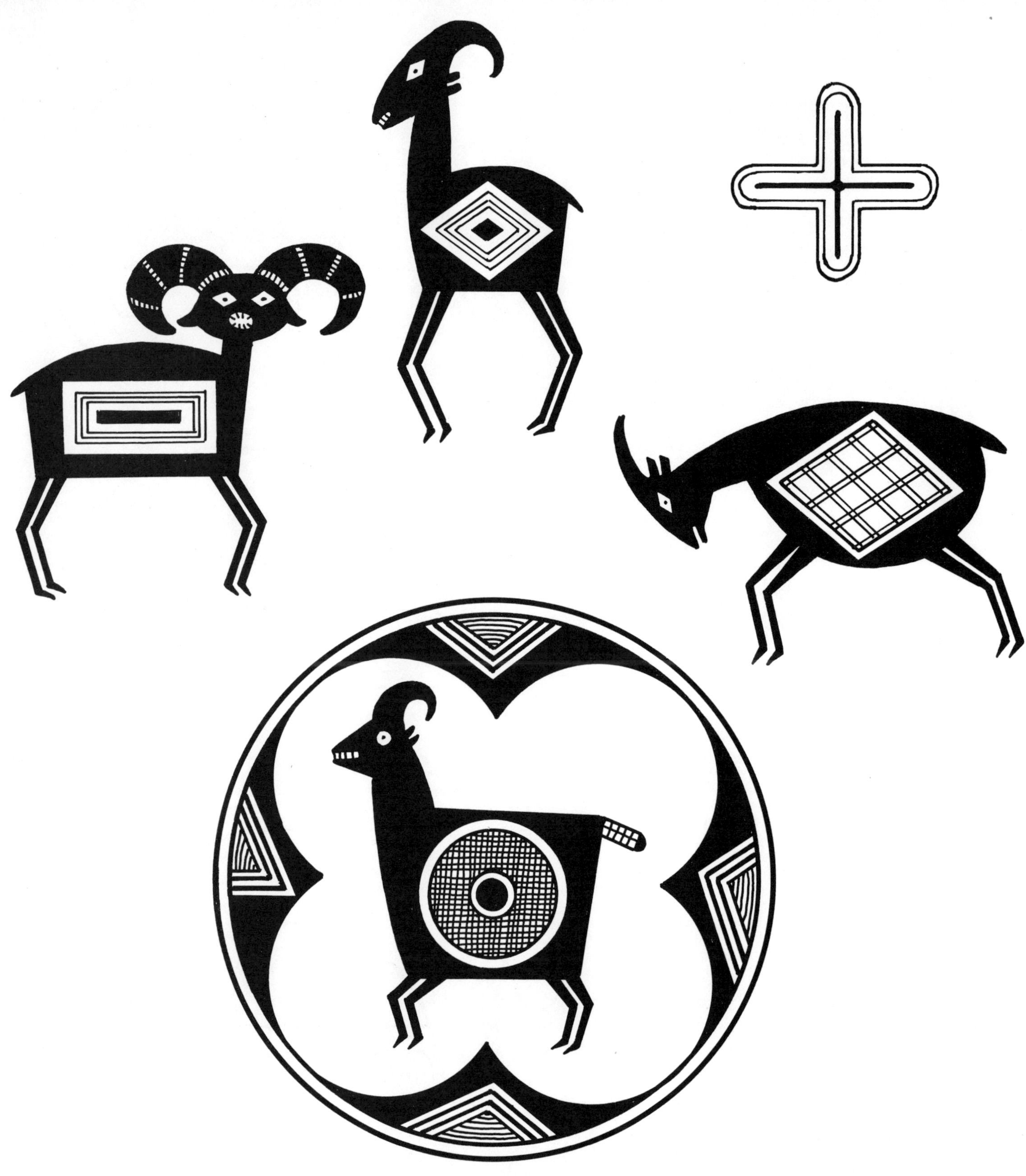

Wild goats and sheep lived in the mountains on either side of the Valley. Their horns are not at all like those of the deer or antelope on the next pages. See how alert they look as they watch for danger. The lower picture shows one painted inside a bowl. In the upper corner is a Mimbres star.

We start with the goat's body, usually drawn as a quadrangle with slanted sides and often a curved top line which is part of a circle.

But it may be made with overlapping circles. Note where circle centers are. And watch that neck—head up if he is running, head down if he is butting.

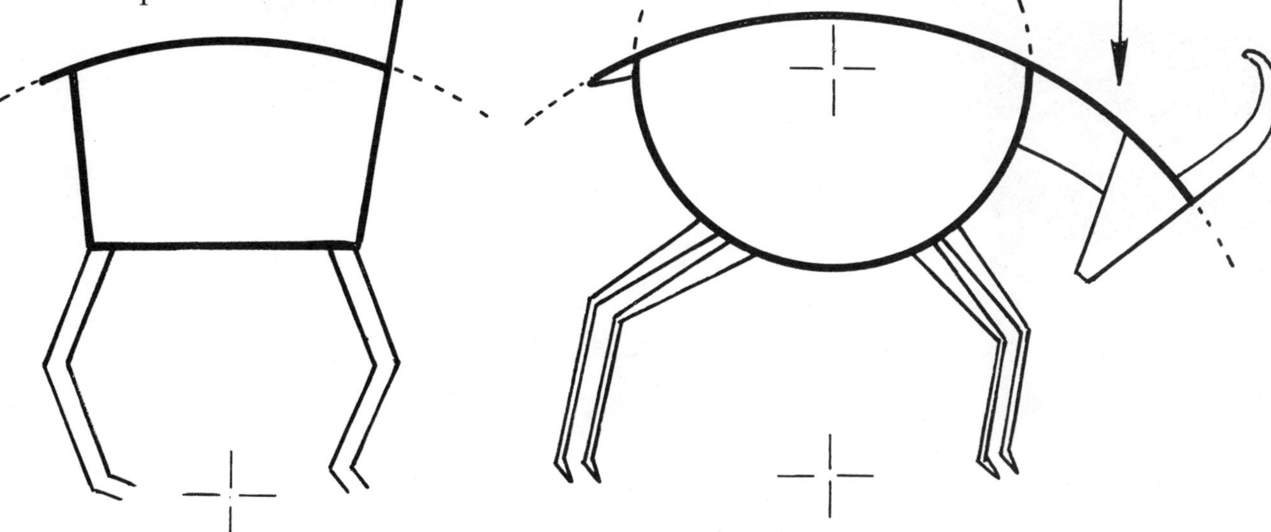

Legs are bent like springs to speed him over the rough mountain side.

Or hind legs may be braced back to give him more pushing power. Show all four legs with sharp hoofs, and add the stubby tail.

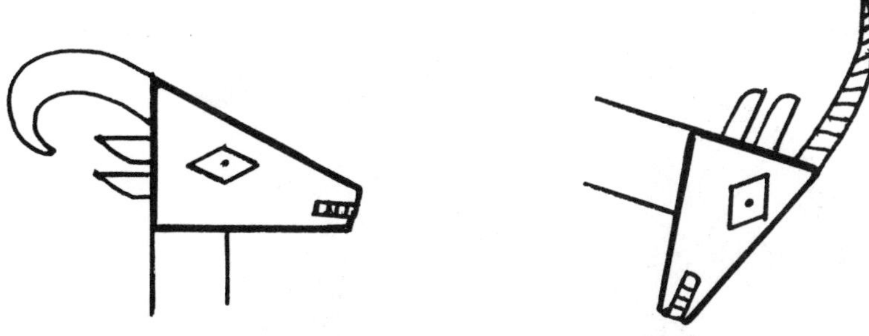

Now, the head. For a side view make it a triangle, with open mouth and big curved horn—much curved for a mountain sheep, straighter for a goat. Ears are small, eyes are usually diamond shaped.

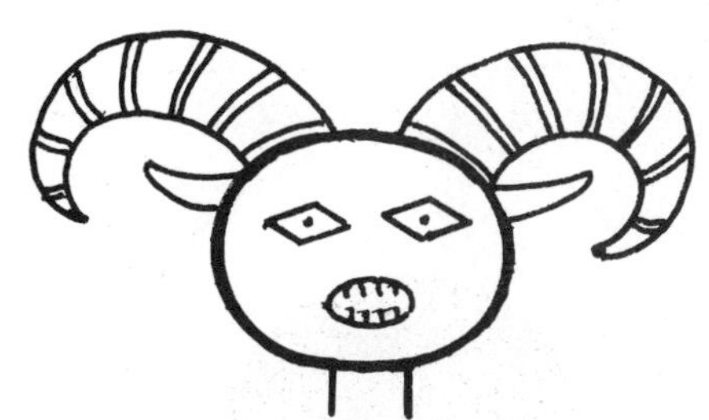

If you want your sheep or goat to look straight at you, draw a circle or oval with a round mouth, and show both horns.

Last, the decoration. Here are other designs the potters drew on these animals. Use any of them, or make up your own, then fill in the black spaces.

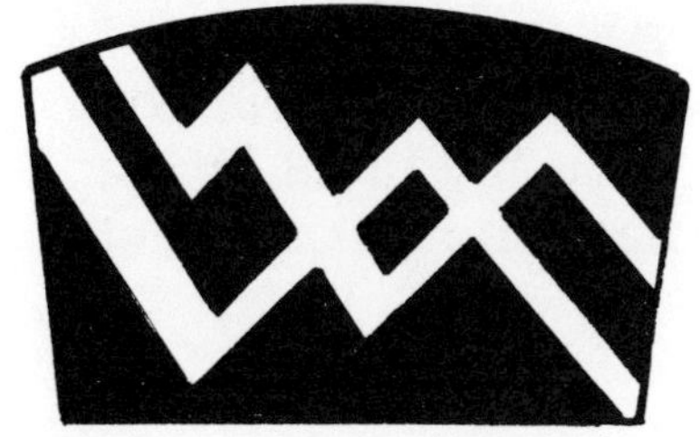

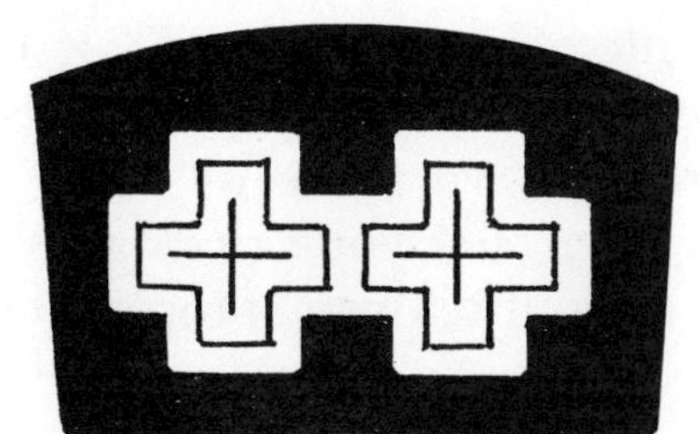

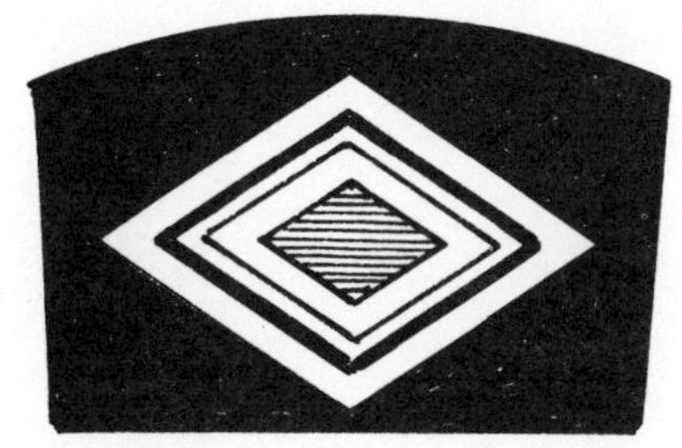

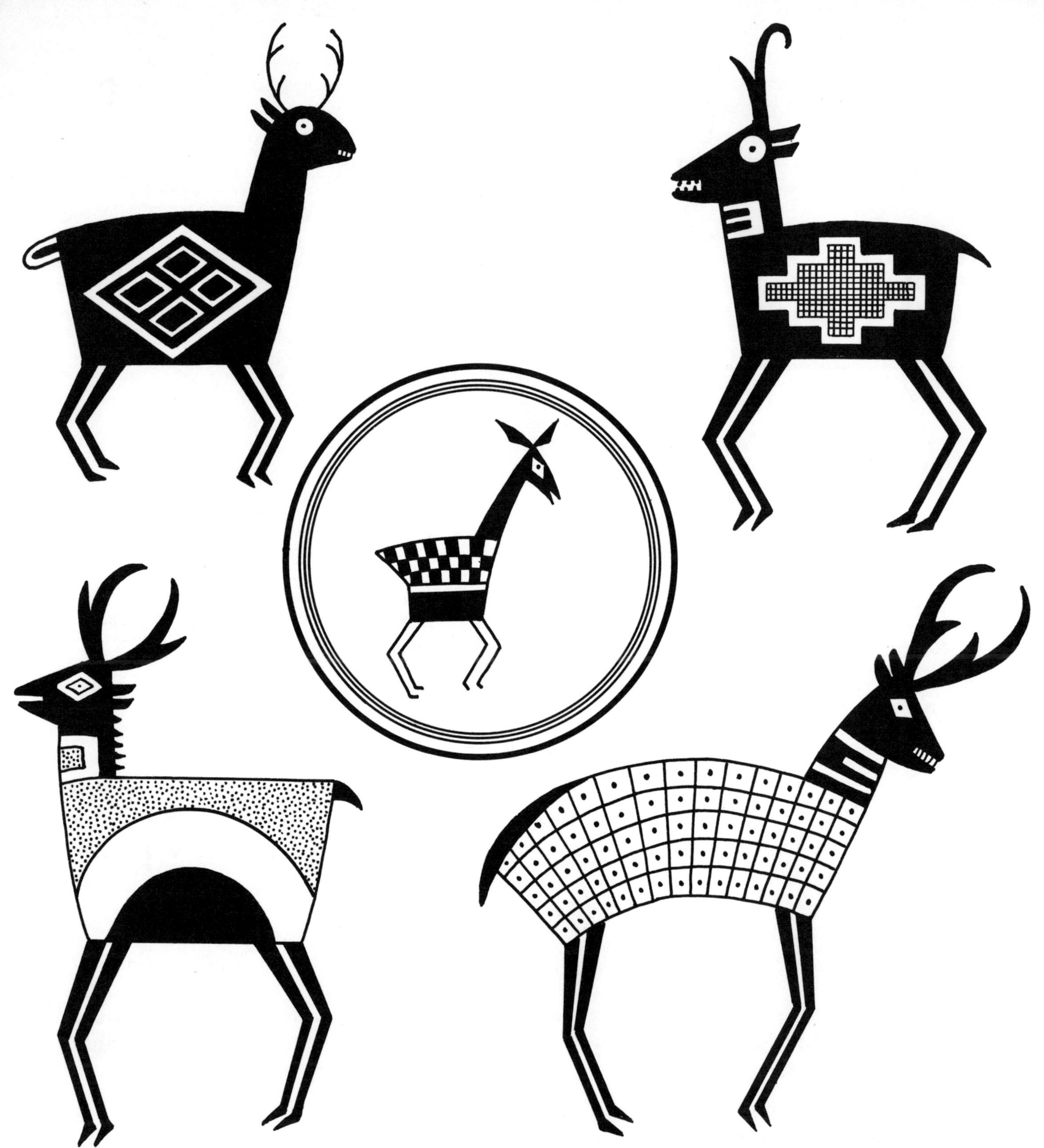

The antelope that grazed on the lower slopes and the flat grasslands had two-pronged horns. Mule deer, shown in the upper corner, have three or more prongs. The little one in the center is a fawn, too young to have horns. Their long legs are bent as though to bound away at top speed.

Now that you have drawn the mountain goat, the deer and antelope should be quite easy.

Starting again with the body, you will see that these creatures are similar to goats, but the Mimbreños never drew them with head lowered. The most notable difference is in the horns.

The deer with it's many-pronged horns has a more rounded and gentle-looking head which you can draw as almost a half-circle, with a round eye. The tail suggests that this is a White Tailed Deer.

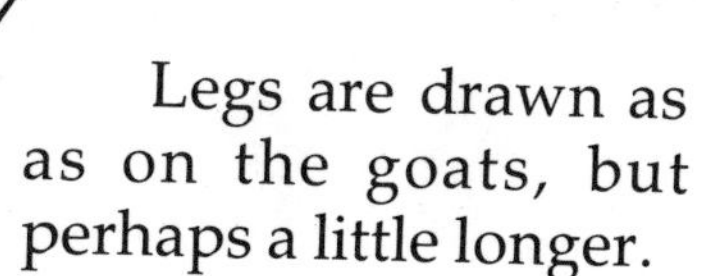

Legs are drawn as as on the goats, but perhaps a little longer.

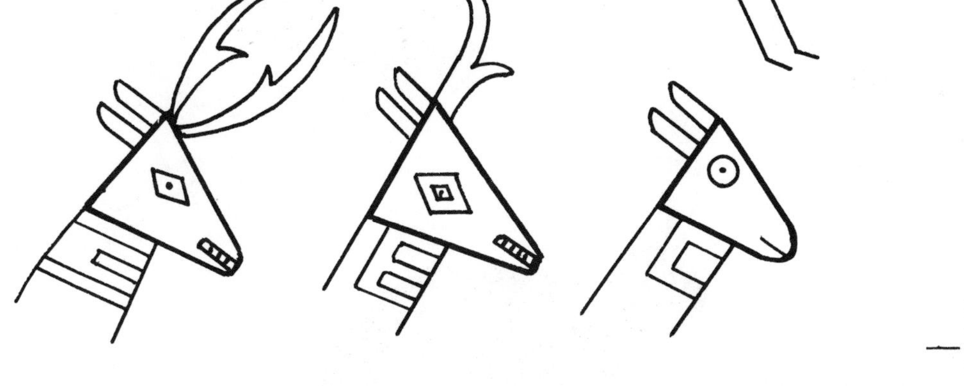

Antelope legs and body are like those of the deer, but the horns are two-pronged and the head is more triangular like the goat's. The throat has white lines suggesting light hair, and the eyes are of various shapes. The doe, or mother deer, has no horns. The big antelope in the lower right corner has the Indian corn symbol all over, showing that he has raided a cornfield.

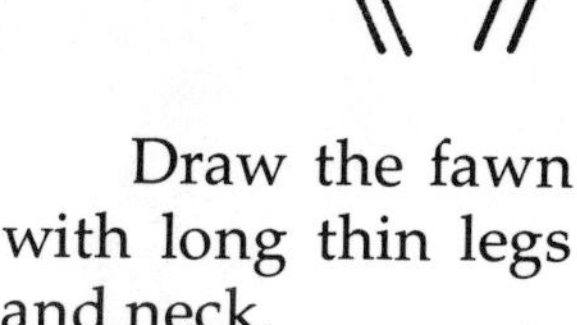

Draw the fawn with long thin legs and neck.

These are other designs the Mimbres potters drew on antelope and deer.

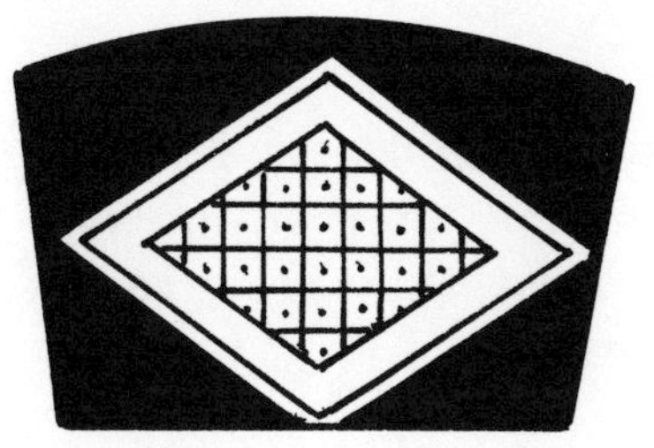

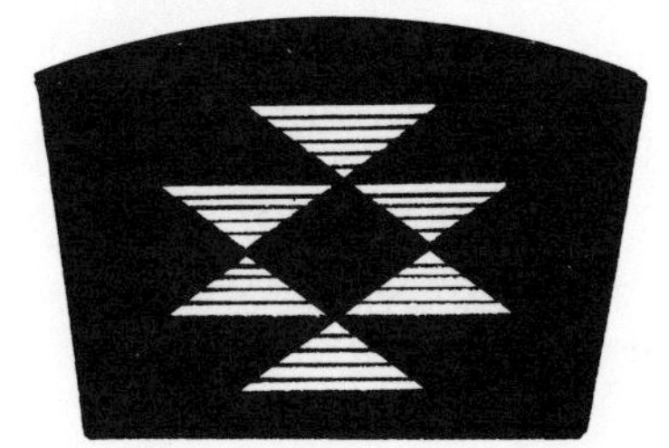

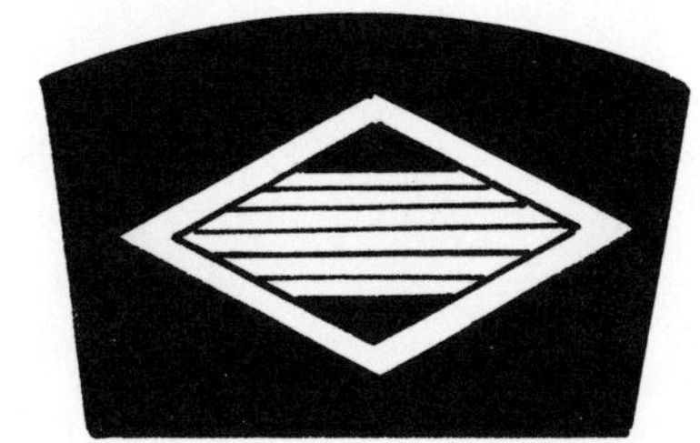

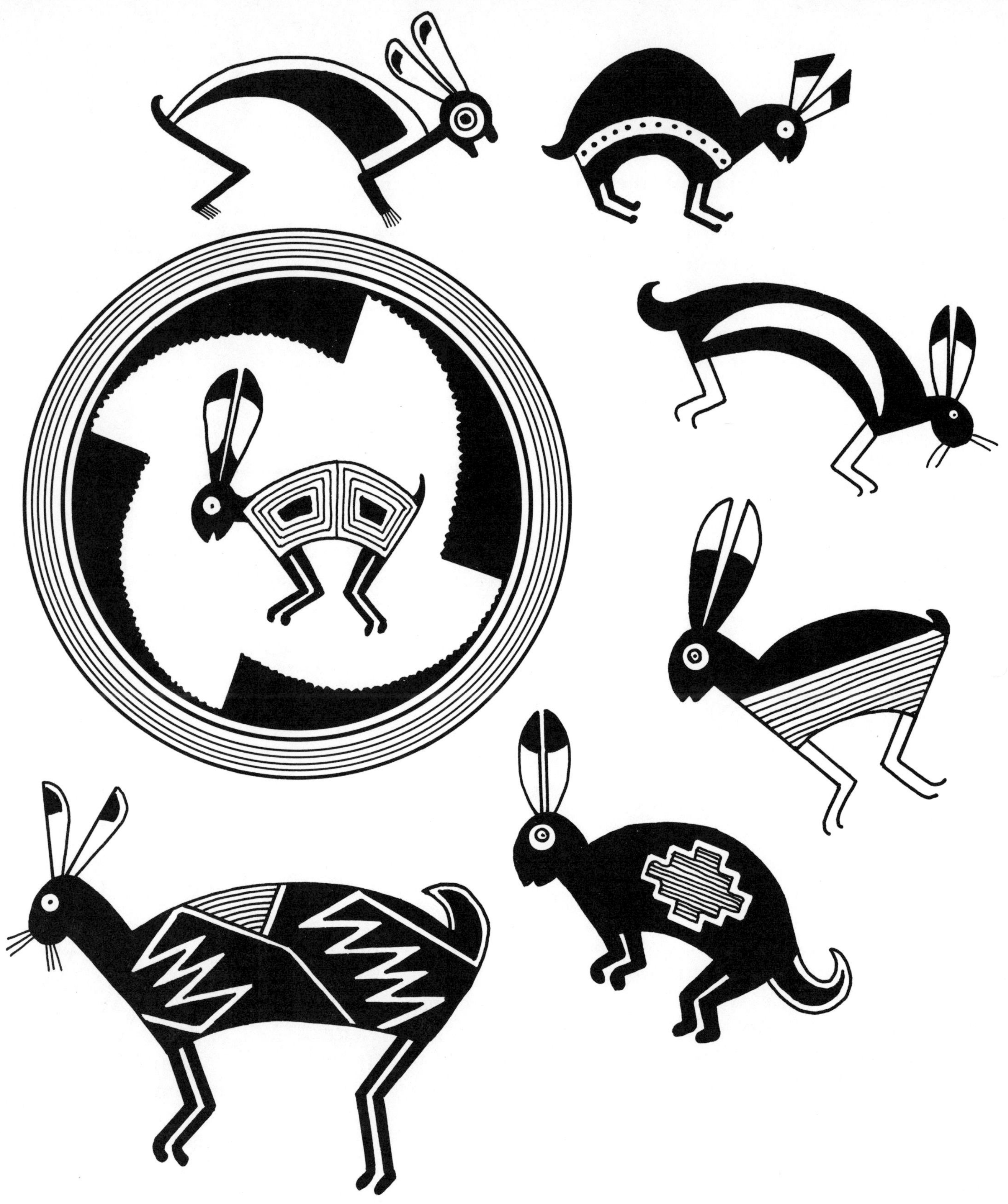

Rabbits were plentiful in the Valley, as they still are. These were long-legged Jack rabbits, not plump little Easter bunnies. Though they could run very swiftly when pursued, they preferred to keep out of sight by scuttling low in the tall grass.

Here we have rabbits and more rabbits in many sizes and shapes.

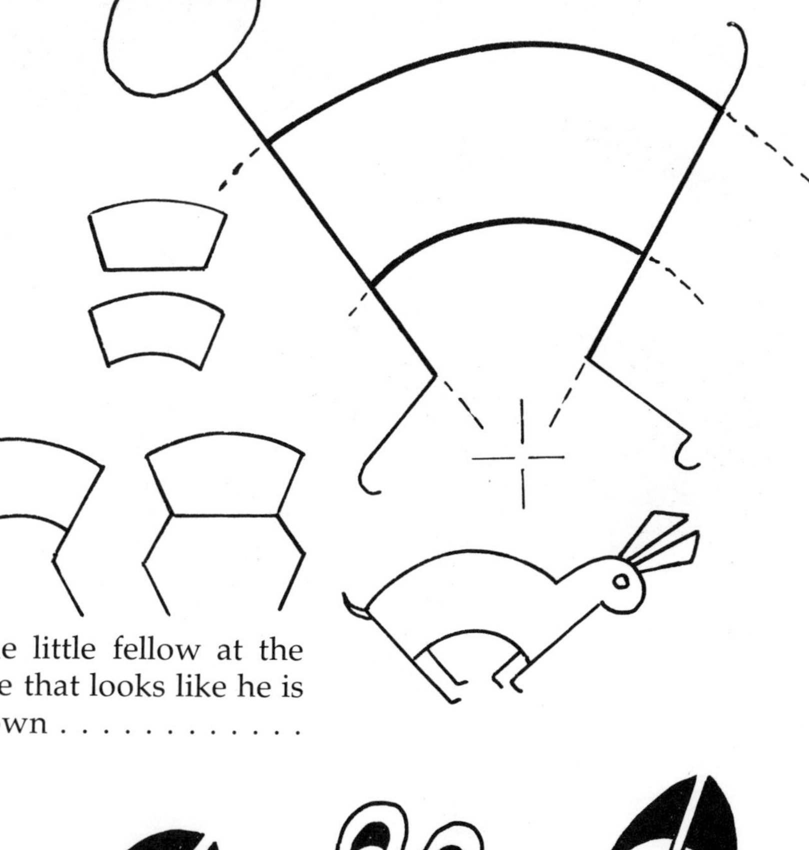

You will remember drawing goats and deer with backs arched but with a straight line below . . . .

These rabbits, however, are drawn with both lines arched, so they look to be hurrying.

Also, all have legs that angle inward instead of out,

except one little fellow at the top of the page that looks like he is going to sit down . . . .

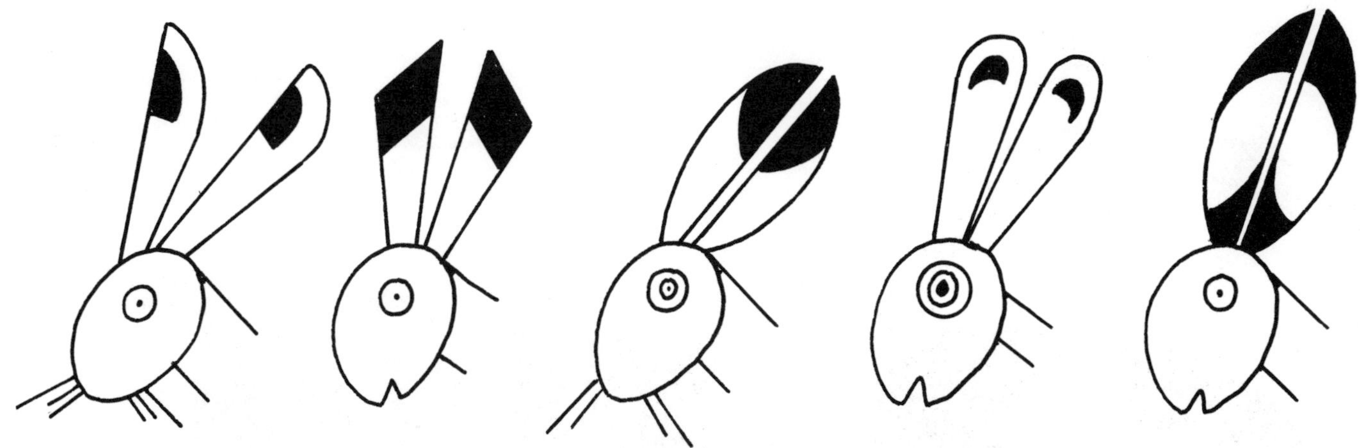

To draw the head, start with an egg-shape on a short neck. The ears are long, held high if he is surprised, laid back if he is hiding. Eyes are round, the small mouth may be open, and he may have whiskers. Decorate ears and body as you wish.

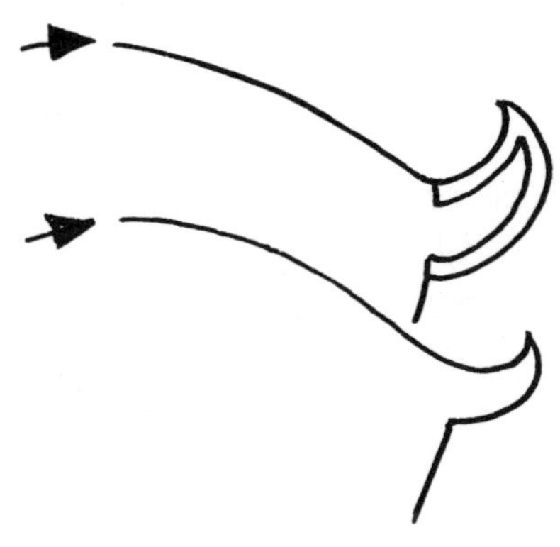

Now we come to the tail. Notice that on some of these rabbits it is drawn by continuing the line of the back upward into a curl; on others it is continuous with the rear line of the body.

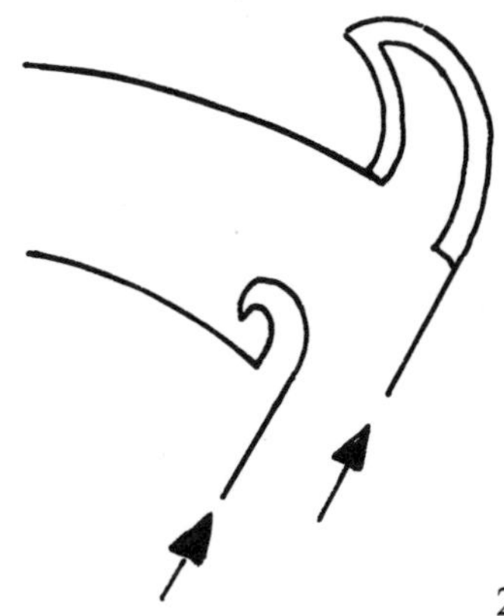

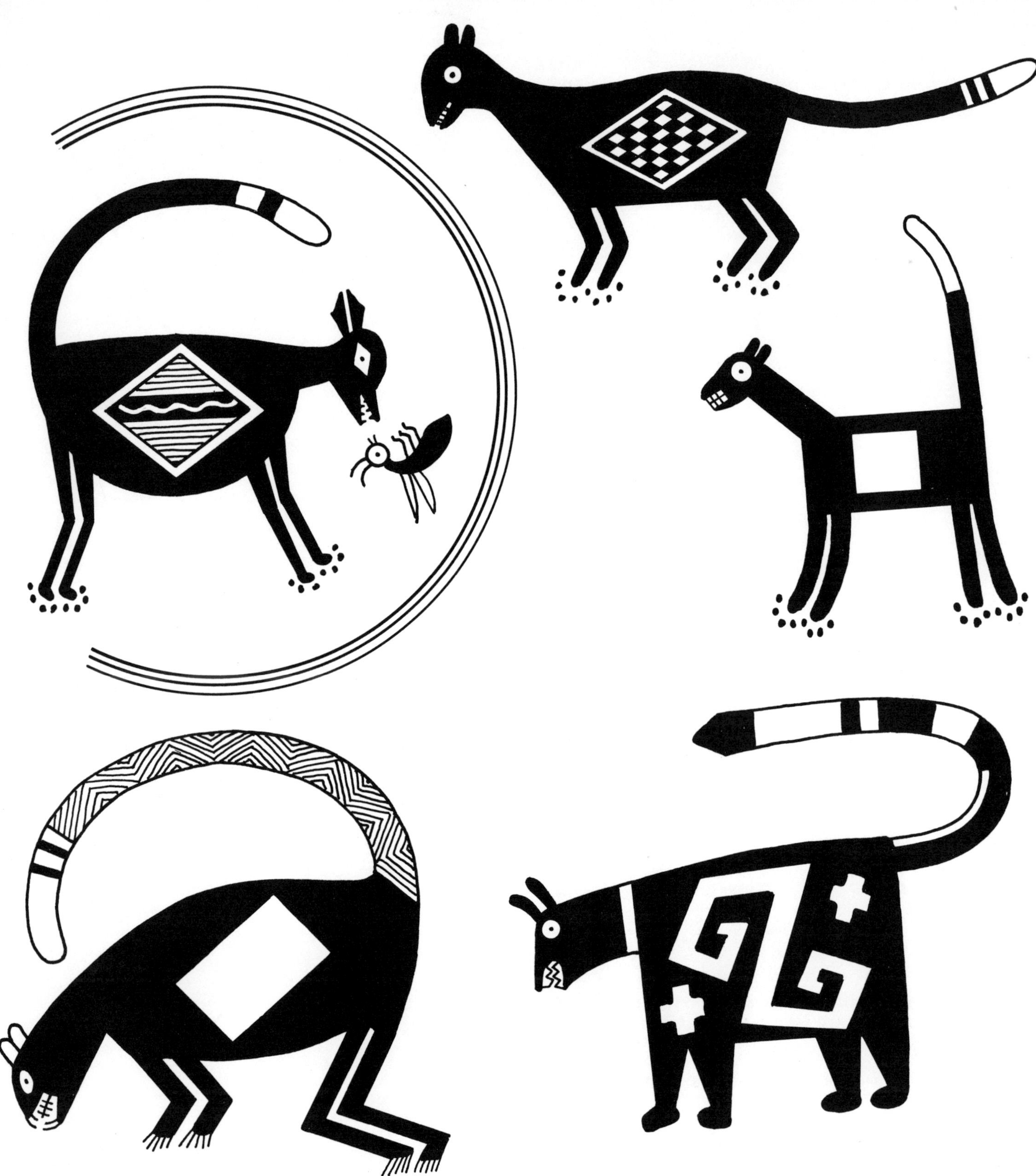

When the Mimbres potters painted the wild cats, ring-tail, mountain lion, or cougar, they usually curled the long tail up over the cat's back. Often the feet were drawn showing the toes. You can see that these animals look ready to pounce, rather than to run away.

Several kinds of wild cats lived in the Valley, so we find them drawn differently. But all have long tails, strong legs, heavy bodies, and plenty of teeth.

For the cat snapping at a bee, start with a circle. The lower half of the circle forms the body, the tail curls about the upper part of the circle. A small circle on a short neck makes the head. Add a toothy snout, ears, four legs with toes, and there is your cat.

This cat also starts with a circle, but his back is curved and extends to form the top of his head. His feet have claws instead of toes, and just look at those wicked teeth! He has the fanciest tail of all.

Now begin with a rectangle. The top line extends to start the head and the loop of the tail and side lines form the outer lines of straight fat legs.

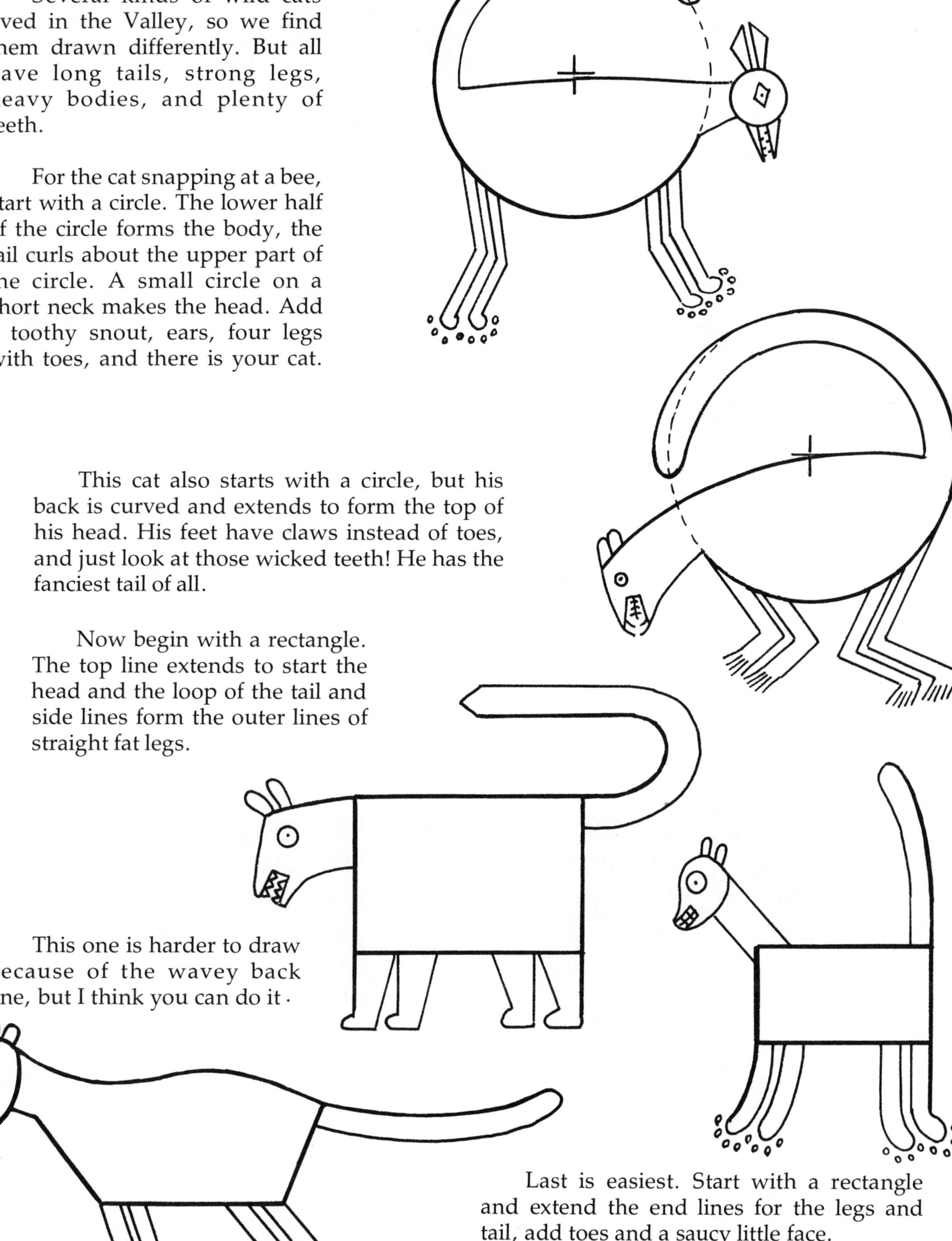

This one is harder to draw because of the wavey back line, but I think you can do it.

Last is easiest. Start with a rectangle and extend the end lines for the legs and tail, add toes and a saucy little face.

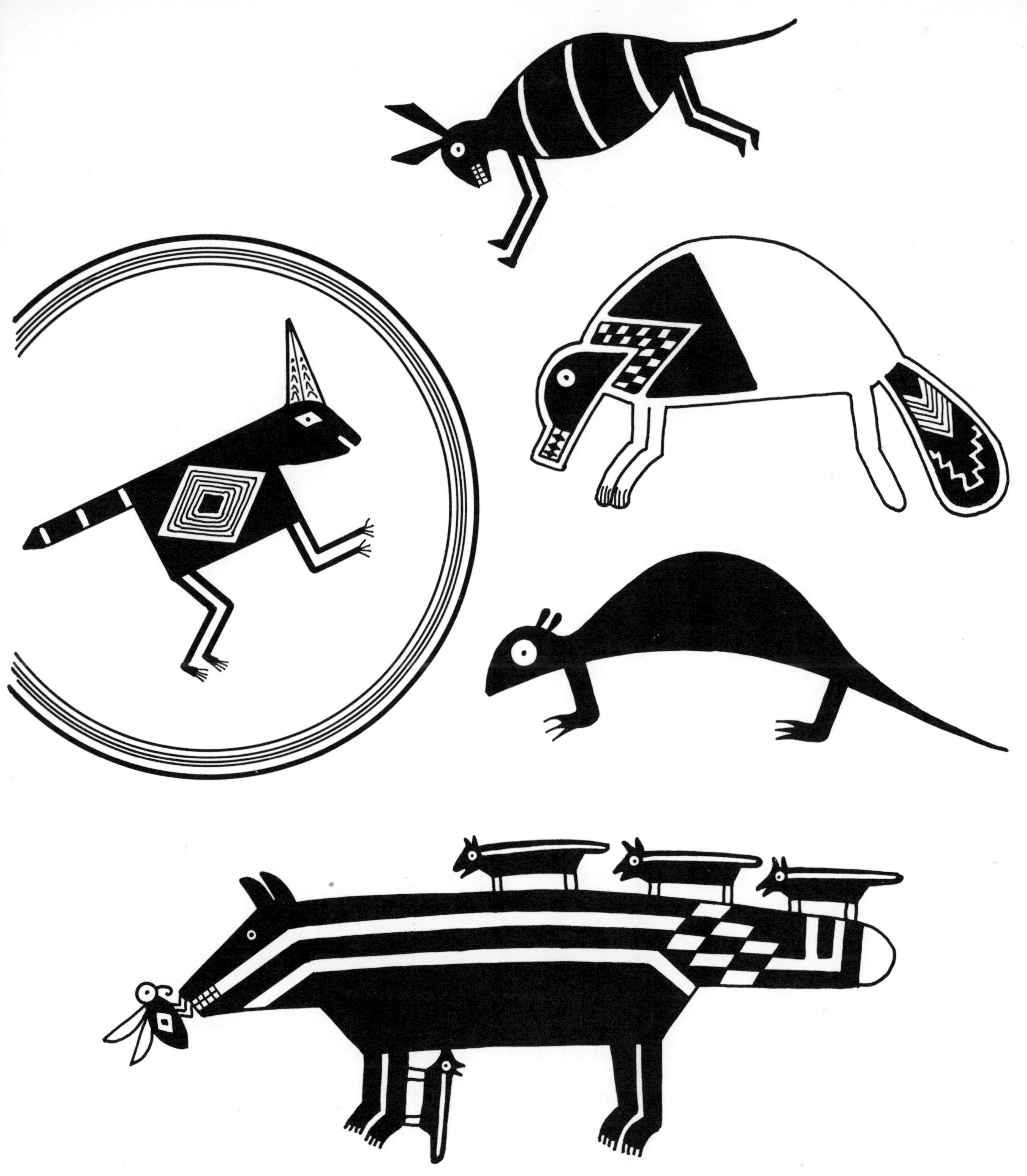

Not all of the animals in the Valley were large. Some small shy creatures lived among the rocks and bushes, in the water or underground. There were the beaver with his wide flat tail, the striped skunk which you see here with her little ones, and many kinds of squirrels, mice, rats and gophers.

The small animals that the Mimbreños drew are often hard to identify. They were drawn in many forms,—squares, half-circles, or with wavey outlines.

This creature with big ears and thin tail might be a wood rat. Try drawing him with two overlapping circles, adding a half-circle head and thin legs and tail.

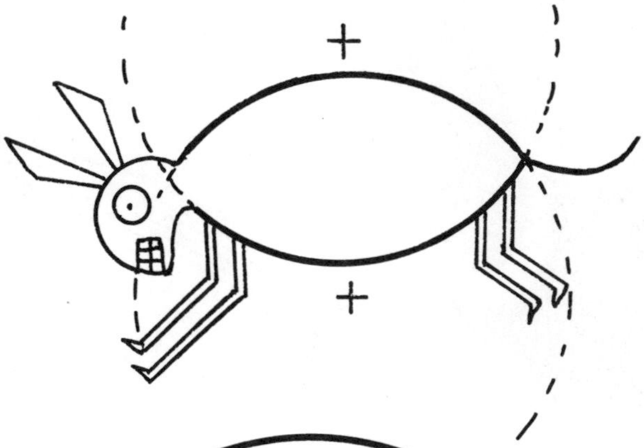

The paddle-shaped tail shows this is a beaver. Again we start with a half-circle but cut off the corners and add head, tail and legs. Note the saw-like teeth for cutting down trees to build dams.

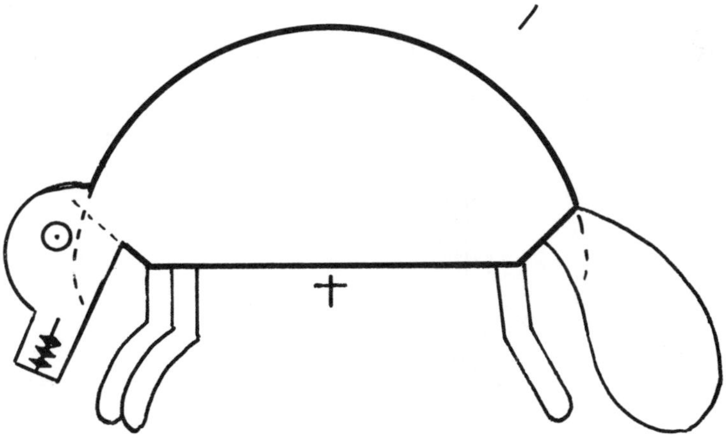

The potter who drew this animal may have meant it for a ferret or a weasel, as they hump their backs like this when running. Start with a wavey line for the back, then a curve for the underside.

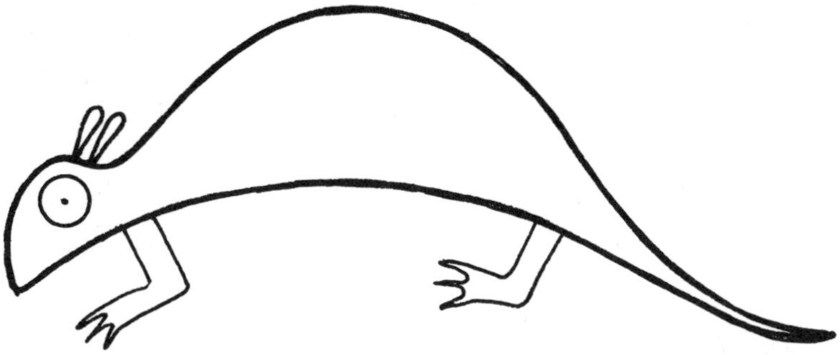

The white stripes mark this as a skunk. Start him with a quadrangular body, the head joining it without a neck. These animals hunt at night, eating many harmful insects and the little ones quickly learn to catch their own suppers.

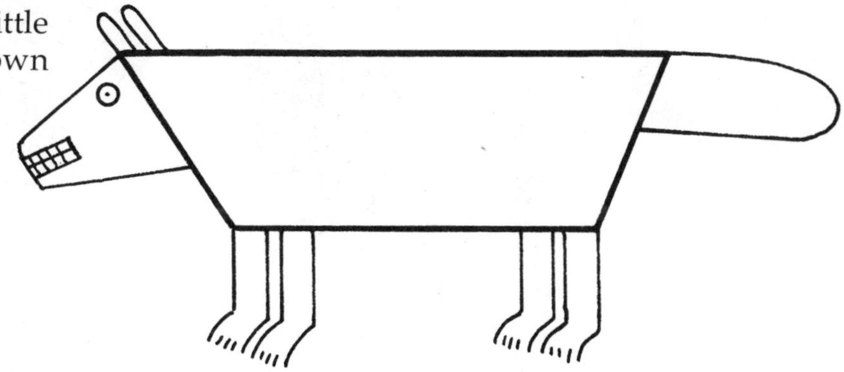

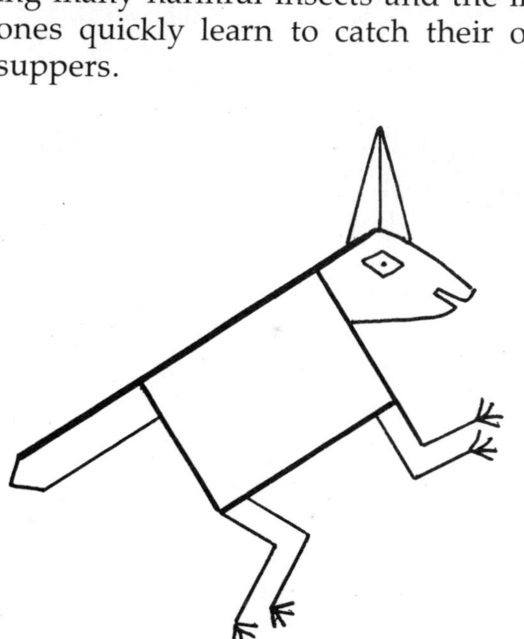

This strange little beast might, because of his pointed ears, be some kind of squirrel. Draw him first as a rectangle, extending the top line to start the head and tail.

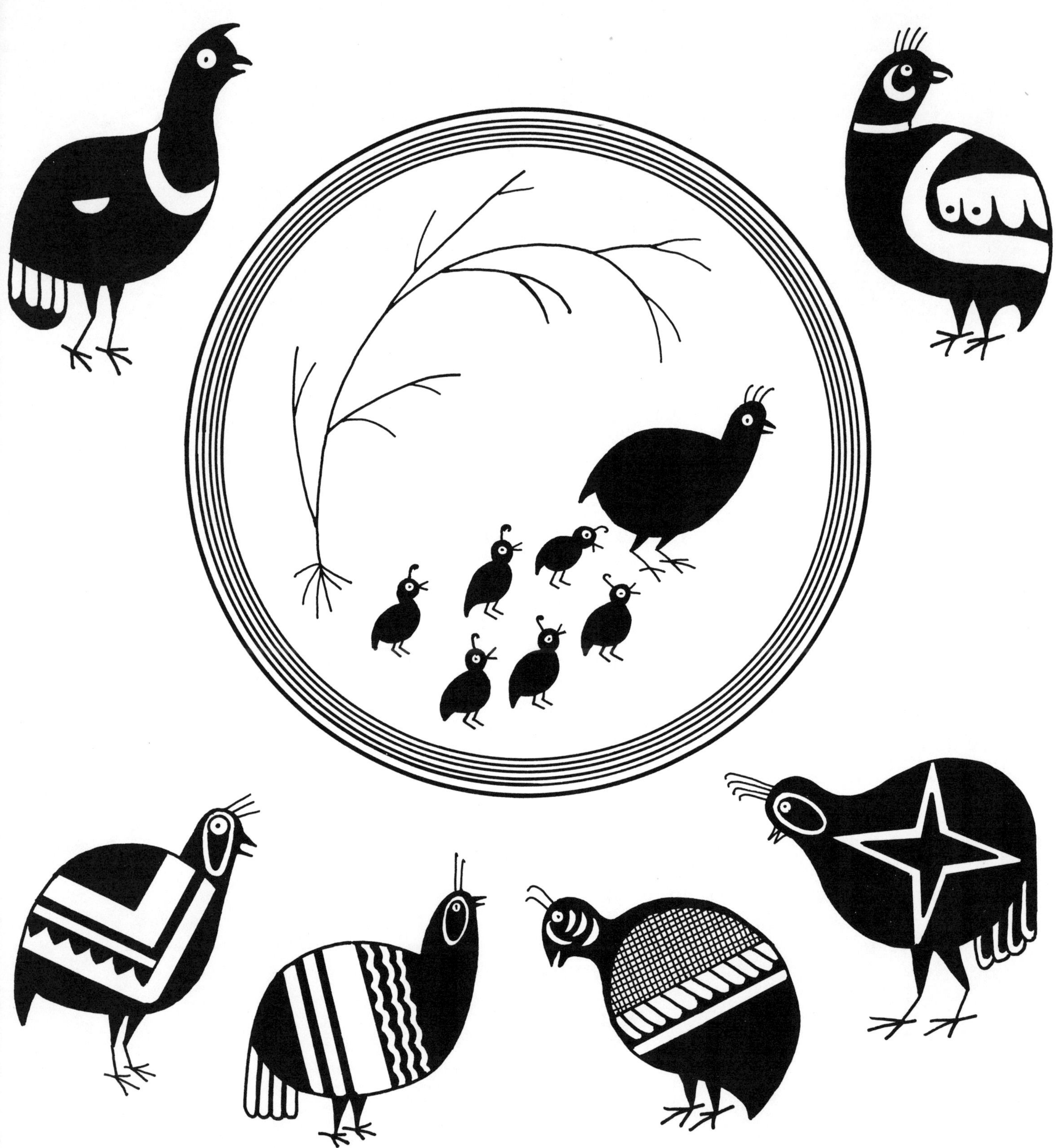

I think the Mimbreños must have liked the little quail very much, as they drew them so often. There are still many of these birds in the Valley, running through the grass on their short legs, with their feather top-knots bobbing as they go, anxiously hiding their chicks from danger.

These small chicken-like birds make their home in dry open country with tall grass or low brush. They can fly, and will perch in trees, but build their nests on the ground.

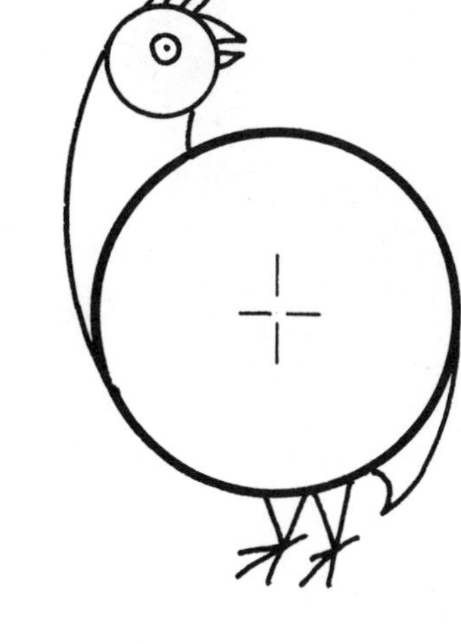

You may start your plump little quail with a circle. Their heads, too, are usually round, on short fat necks, and all have top-knots. Most have markings around the eye, and quite fine feather patterns.

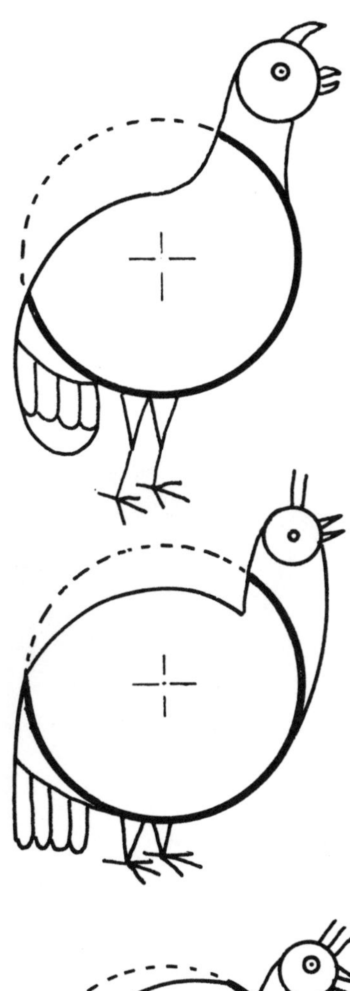

The three birds on the left do not fit exactly into circles, but you can see they are quail because they look so much like the others. The tail may be drawn pointed or as several feathers. As before, you will erase the unused part of the circle before finishing your drawing.

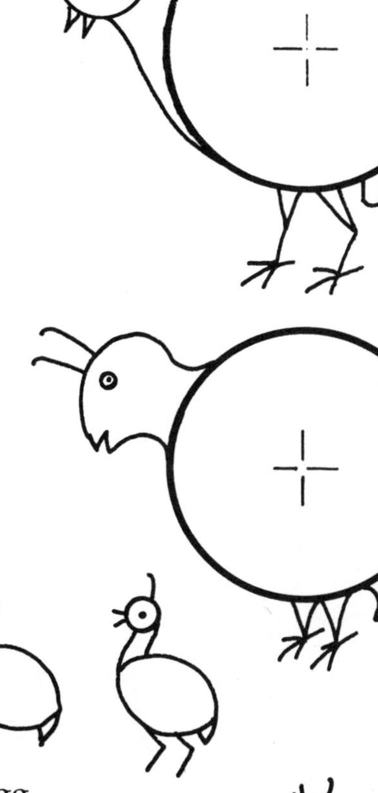

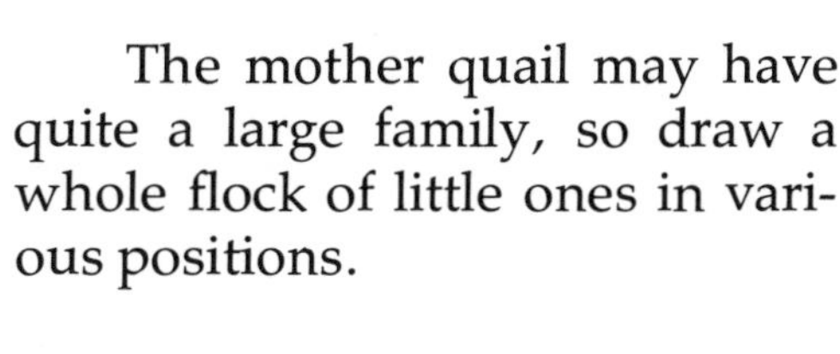

How to hatch a quail egg . .

The mother quail may have quite a large family, so draw a whole flock of little ones in various positions.

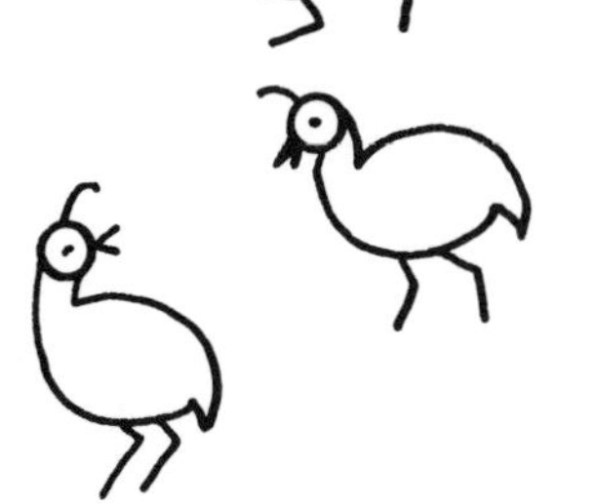

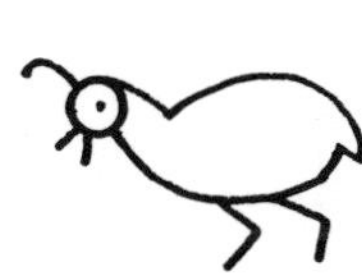

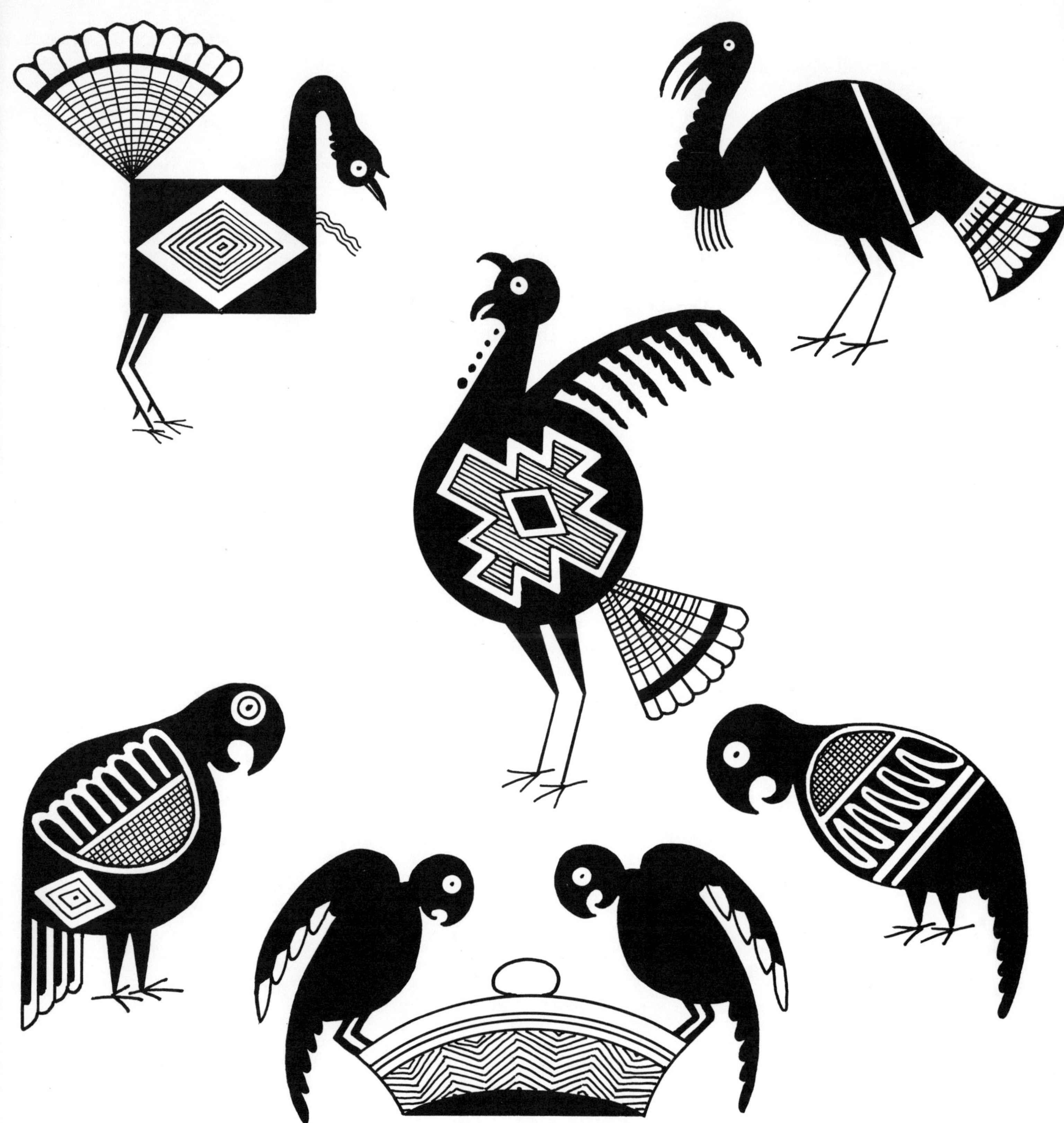

Turkeys and parrots were valued for their feathers, which were used in many ways. Wild turkeys lived in the wooded foothills, but the parrots were raised and trained in the villages. Notice the wattles and the proud tails of the turkeys, and the strong curved beaks of the parrots.

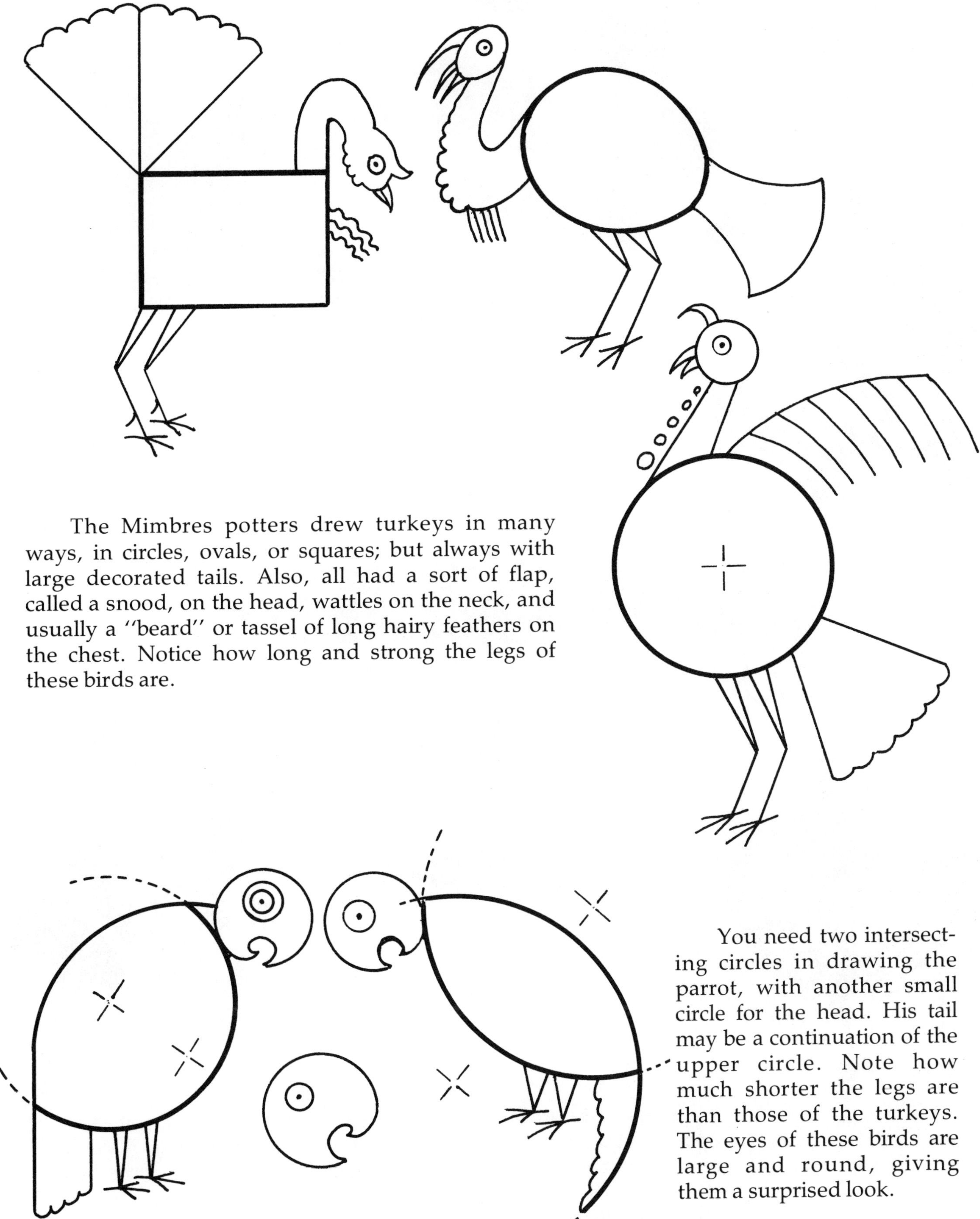

The Mimbres potters drew turkeys in many ways, in circles, ovals, or squares; but always with large decorated tails. Also, all had a sort of flap, called a snood, on the head, wattles on the neck, and usually a "beard" or tassel of long hairy feathers on the chest. Notice how long and strong the legs of these birds are.

You need two intersecting circles in drawing the parrot, with another small circle for the head. His tail may be a continuation of the upper circle. Note how much shorter the legs are than those of the turkeys. The eyes of these birds are large and round, giving them a surprised look.

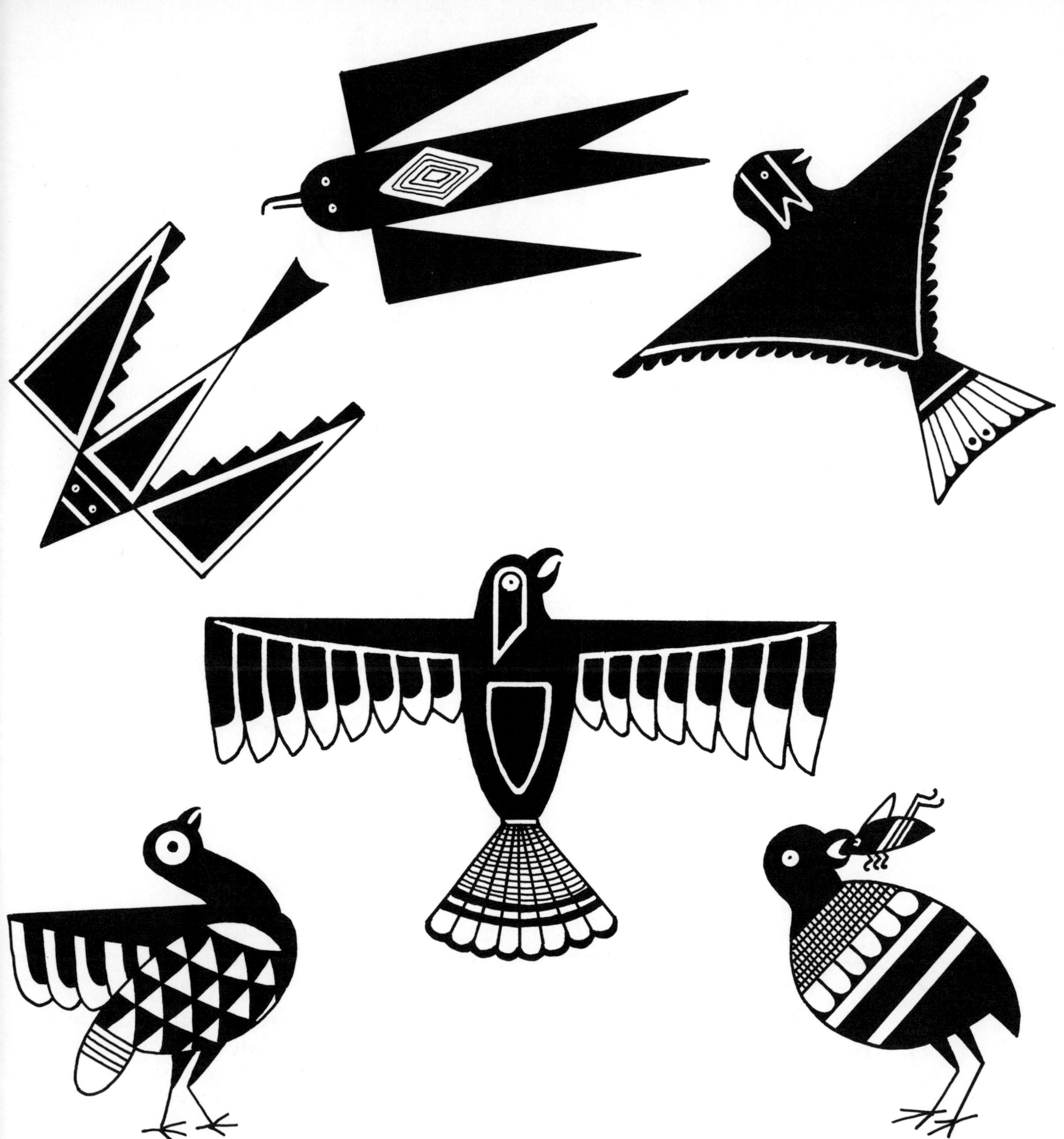

Birds were often drawn with wings spread as in flight. The upper group are probably swallow, doves, sparrow, or such small birds. The center one may be a hawk or eagle. Below are two standing birds, one with wings lifted as if ready to take off, the other breakfasting on a grasshopper.

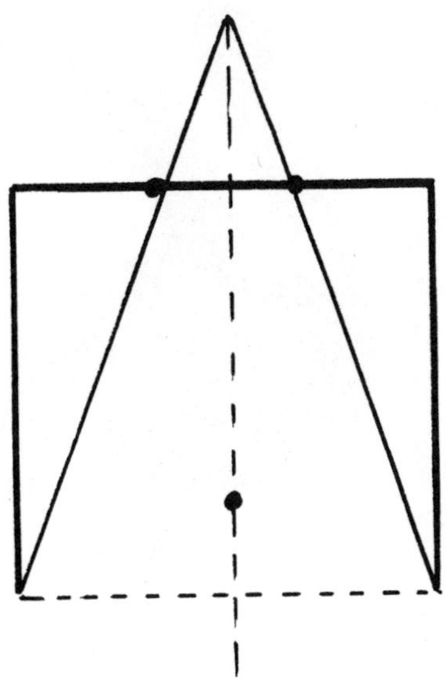

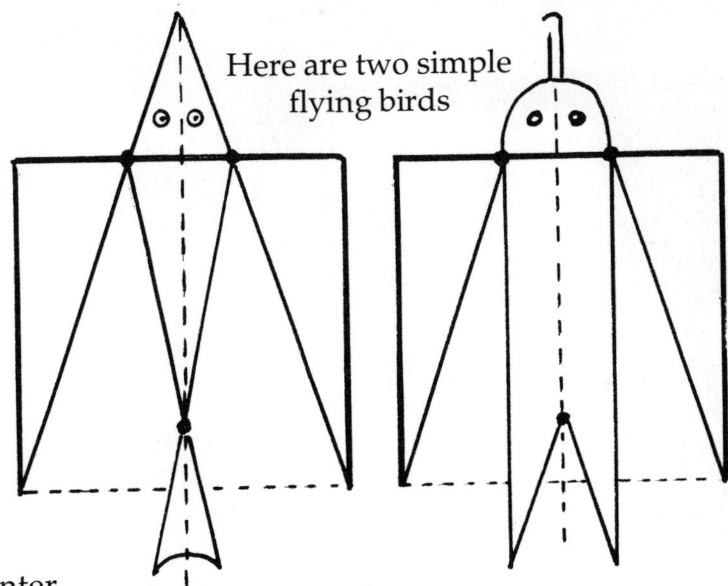

Start with a square, add a vertical center line. Divide top line into three equal parts with dots. Draw lines from lower corners of square through dots on top line. For first bird, continue lines to form head and beak; mark dot on center line a little way from bottom of square and form body with lines between the three dots, extending lines to form tail. Now try the second flying bird.

Here we start in a square laid cornerwise and add a center line from corner to corner. Curved lines inside the square form wings, while the tail is mostly outside the square.

This big Thunderbird also begins with a cornerwise square. Notice carefully where neck, wing tips, and tail are within the square.

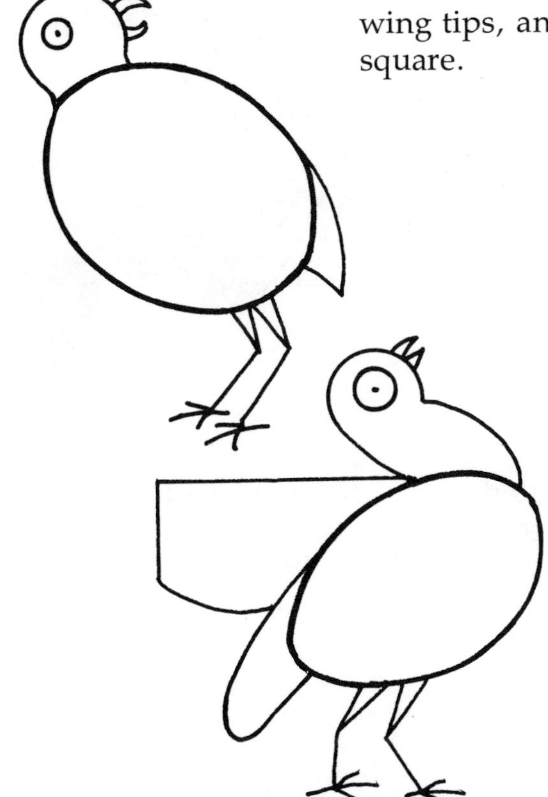

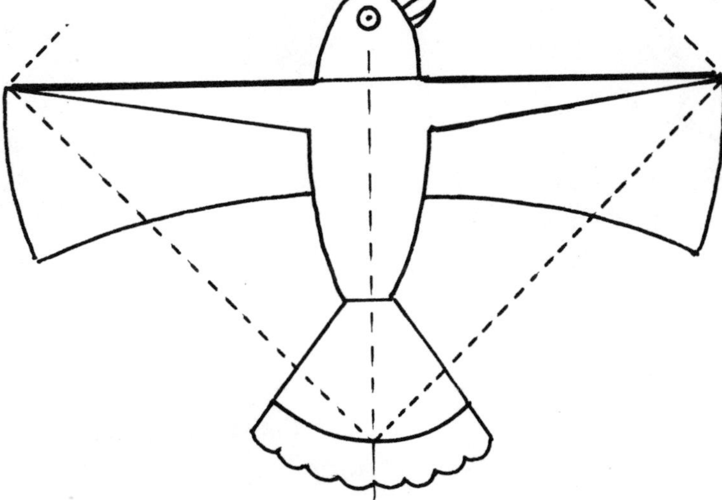

The two standing birds start as egg-shapes. In adding designs on all of these birds, notice the eyes are always round, and many of the decorations look like over-lapping feathers.

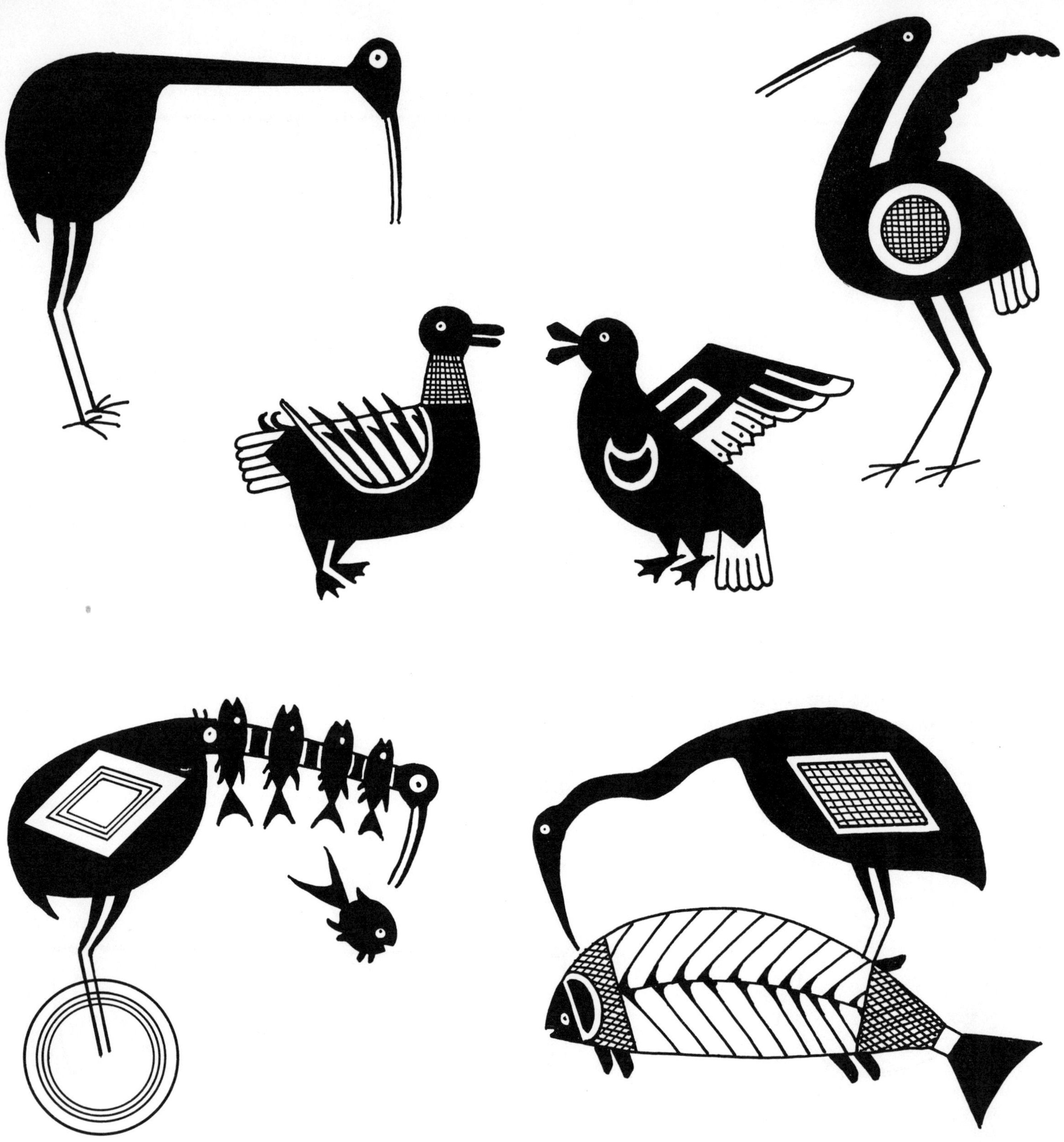

Fish-eating water birds nested along the river banks. Their long legs and beaks helped them in food gathering, the greedy ones often catching more than they could handle. Another water bird was the duck. See the wide beak, short legs and webbed feet of the pair in the center of the page.

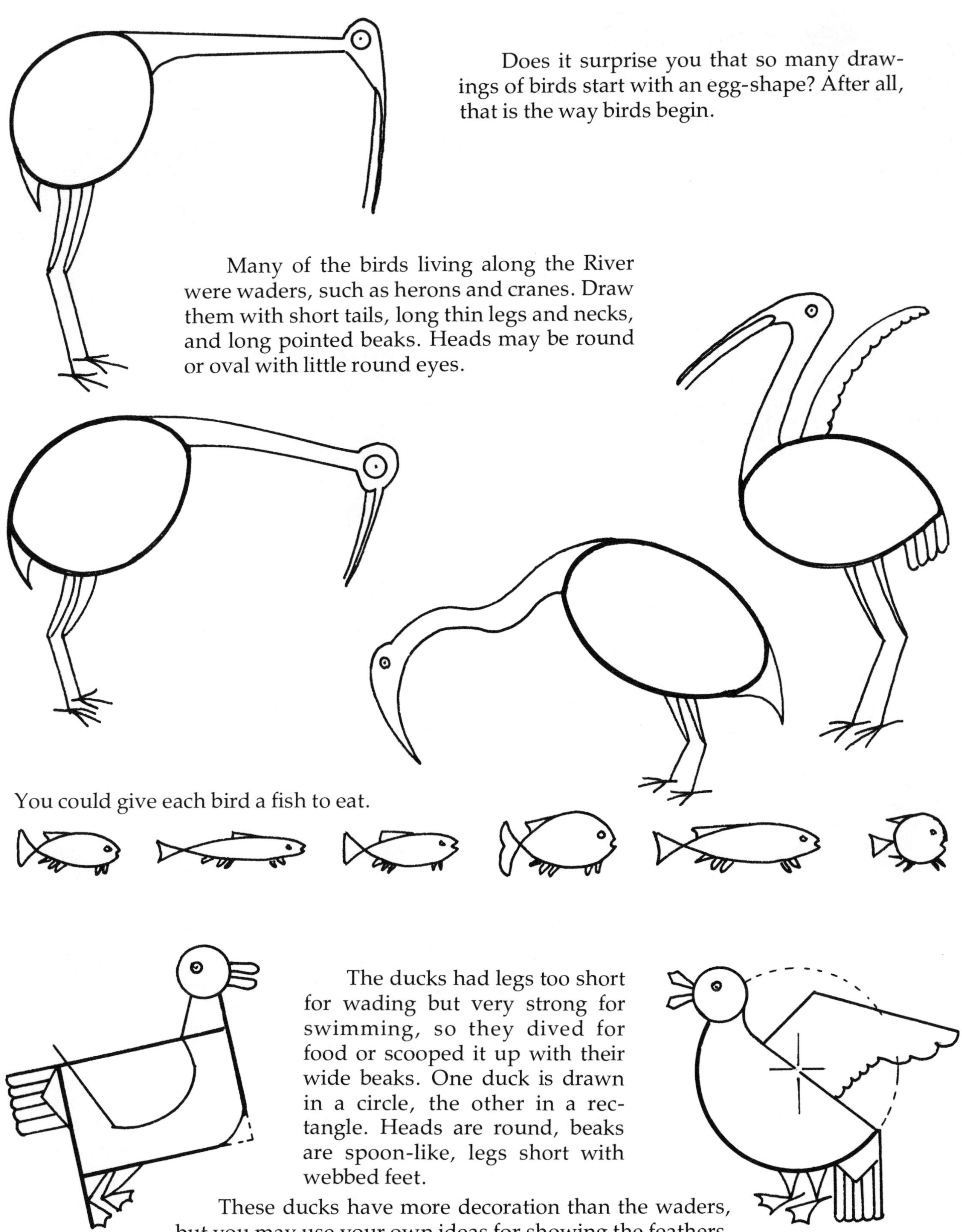

Does it surprise you that so many drawings of birds start with an egg-shape? After all, that is the way birds begin.

Many of the birds living along the River were waders, such as herons and cranes. Draw them with short tails, long thin legs and necks, and long pointed beaks. Heads may be round or oval with little round eyes.

You could give each bird a fish to eat.

The ducks had legs too short for wading but very strong for swimming, so they dived for food or scooped it up with their wide beaks. One duck is drawn in a circle, the other in a rectangle. Heads are round, beaks are spoon-like, legs short with webbed feet.

These ducks have more decoration than the waders, but you may use your own ideas for showing the feathers.

Many kinds of fish swam in the Mimbres River, fat ones like sunfish or bluegills, slender ones like trout, as well as catfish, minnows, and others. The people of the Valley caught them in nets which the women wove from hair or from the fibers of plants.

Fish are among the easiest of all creatures to draw. Let us start with a sunfish—just a circle with a triangle for a tail. Or draw a shape not quite a circle, as those just below. Then add the fins; one above, two pairs and a single one below.

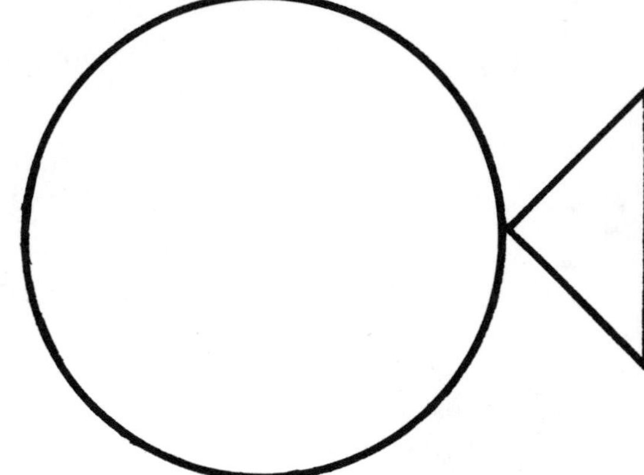

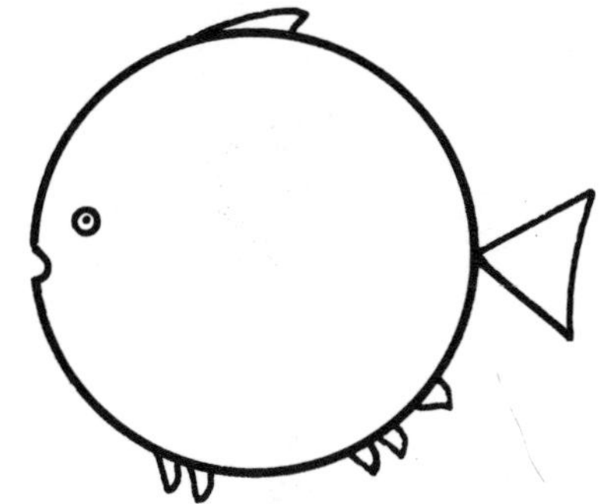

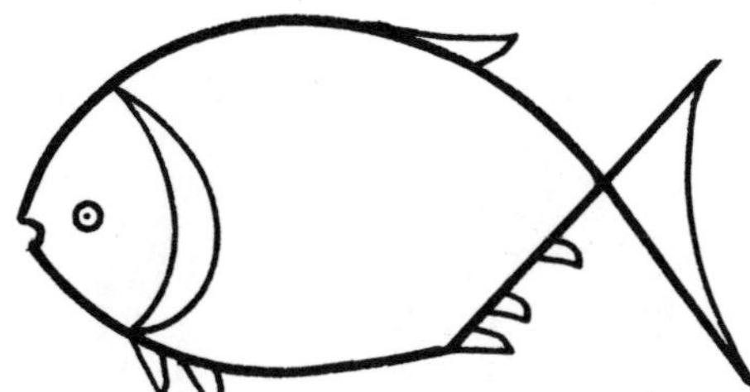

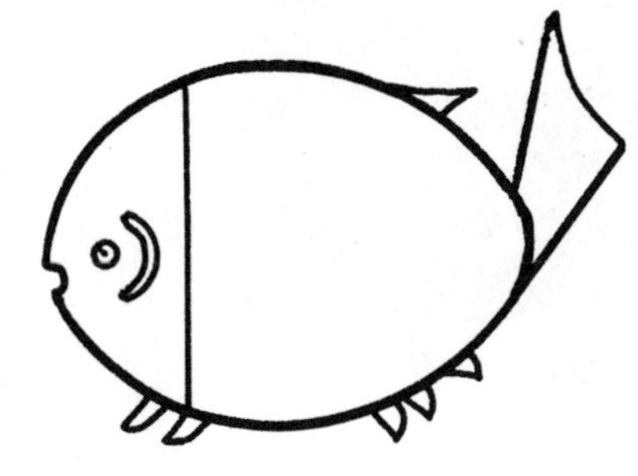

The open mouth is small, eyes usually small and round. • Often there is a half-moon behind the eye, like a gill. • The tail may slant or be not quite a triangle.

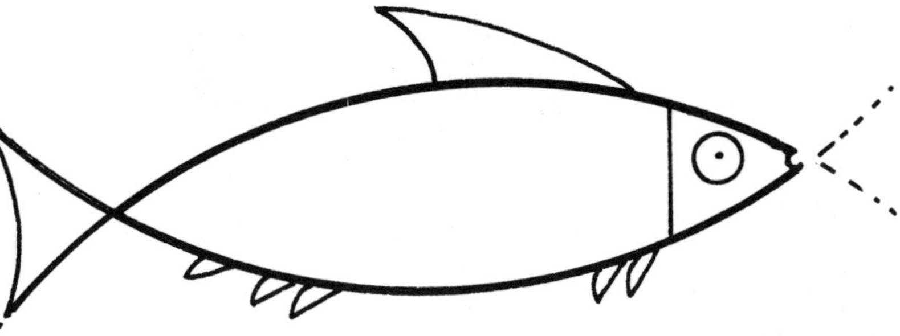

The long slender trout is also easy to draw, starting with two intersecting arcs. The number of fins is the same as on the sunfish.

The interesting features of the catfish are the whiskers and the barb on his head, neither of which we find on trout or sunfish.

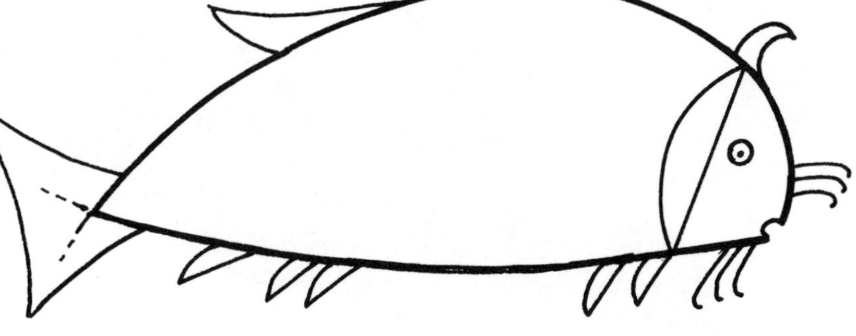

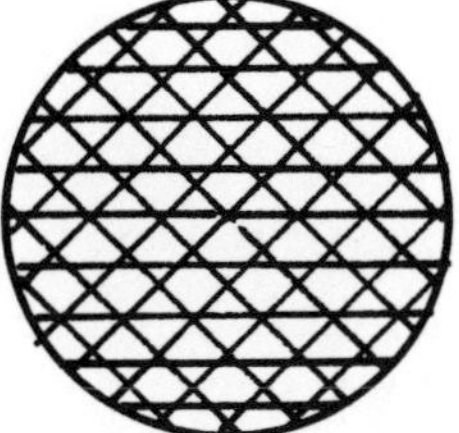

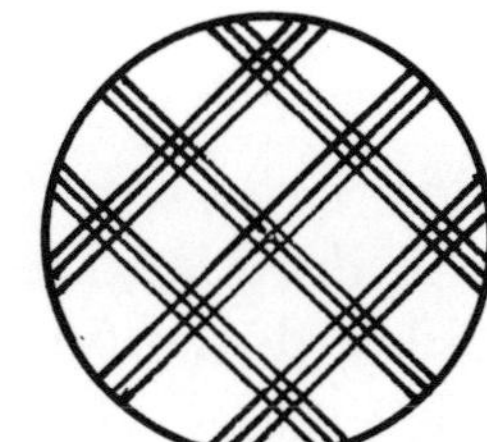

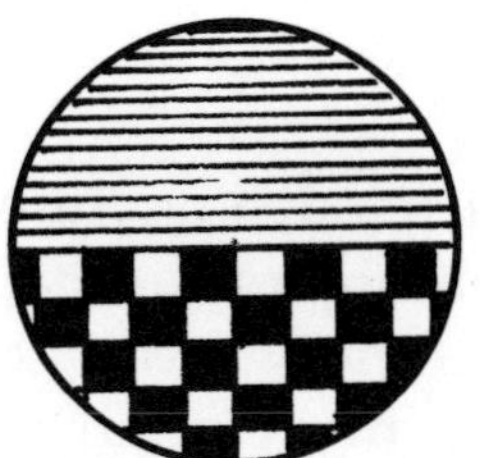

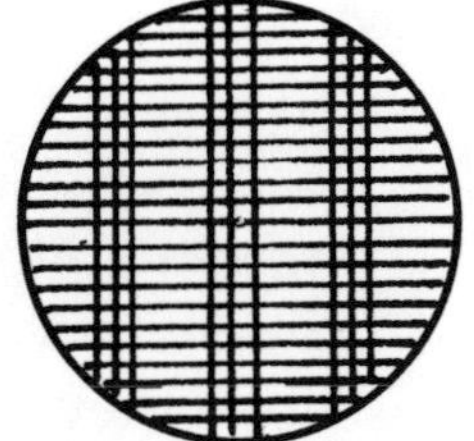

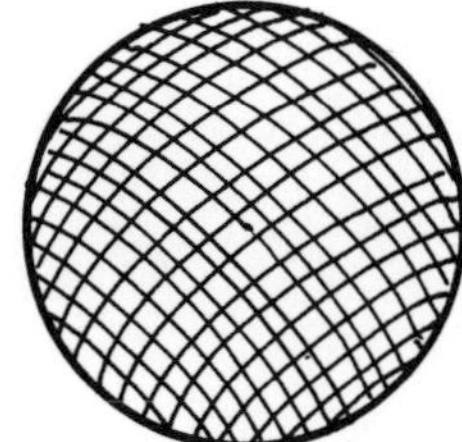

Here are a few of the ways the Mimbres potters indicated scales on fish.

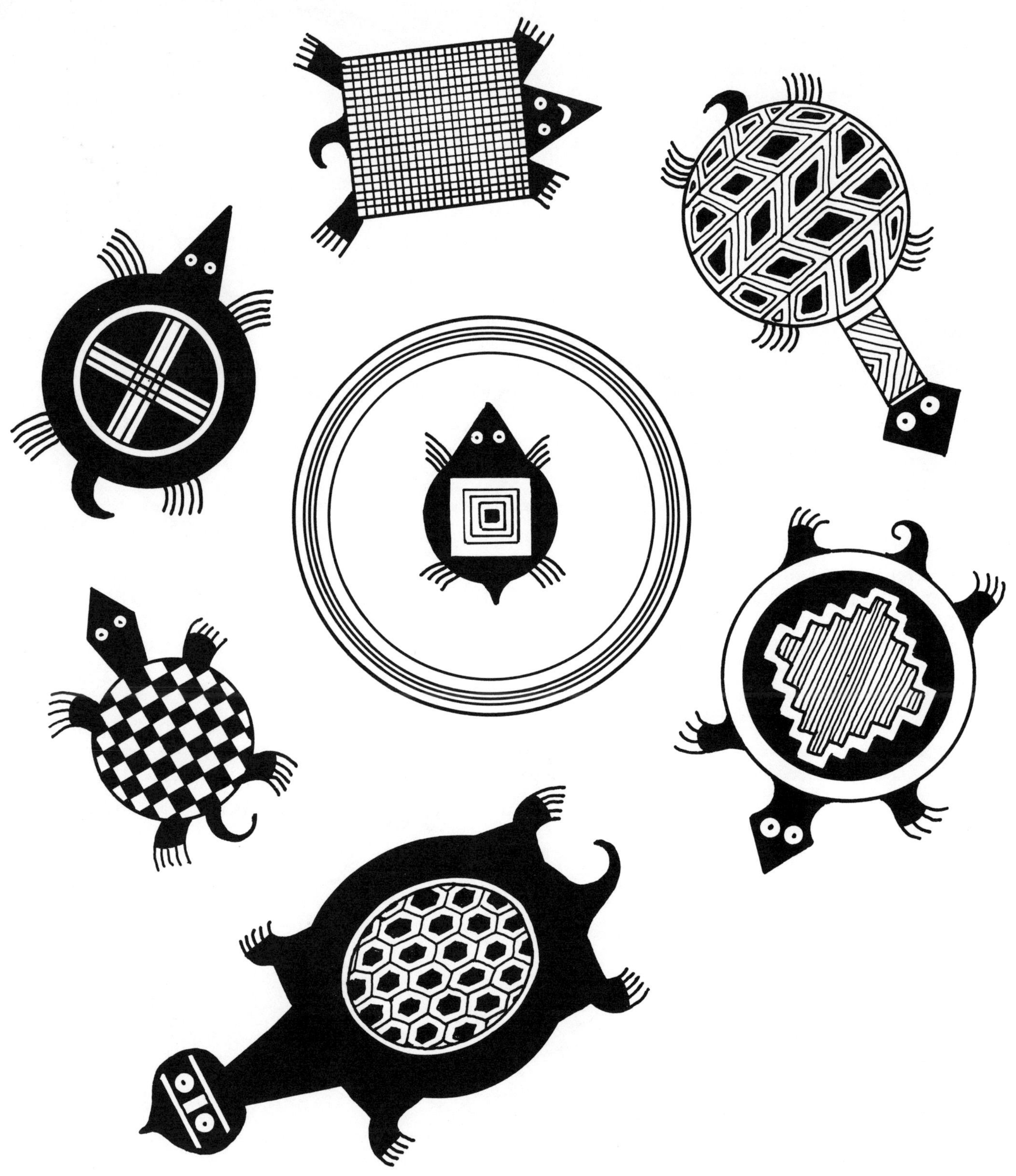

Some turtles, such as mud turtles, lived along the river bank; others preferred higher sandy ground. Both land turtles and water dwellers were drawn as though looking down on them, as that is how they were most often seen. The wide clawed feet served equally well for swimming or crawling.

Turtles come in several shapes. Most are round, but some are oval or square. All shapes have the same short curved tail.

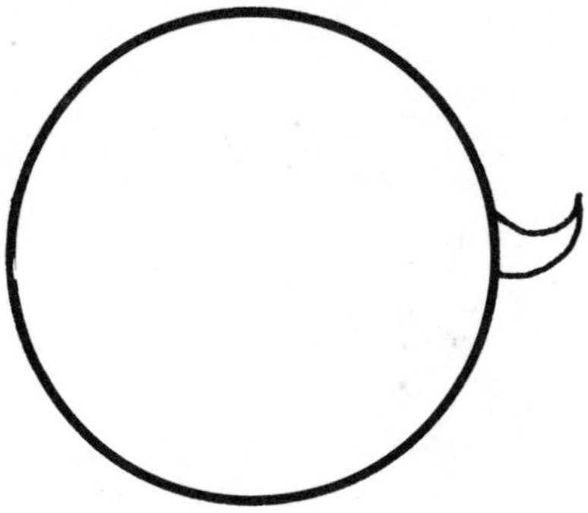

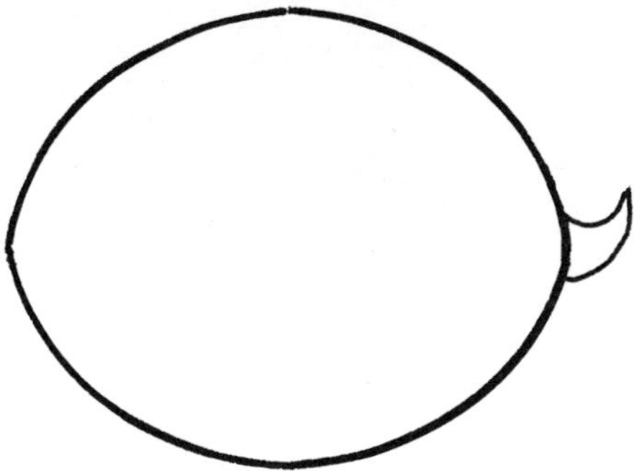

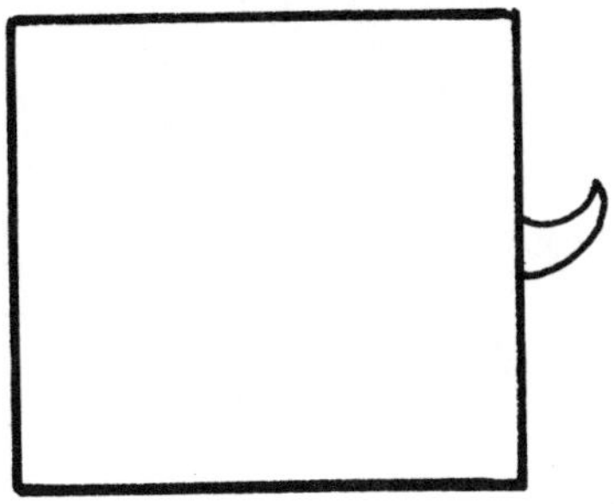

Some of the pointed heads are on long thin necks . . . . . .

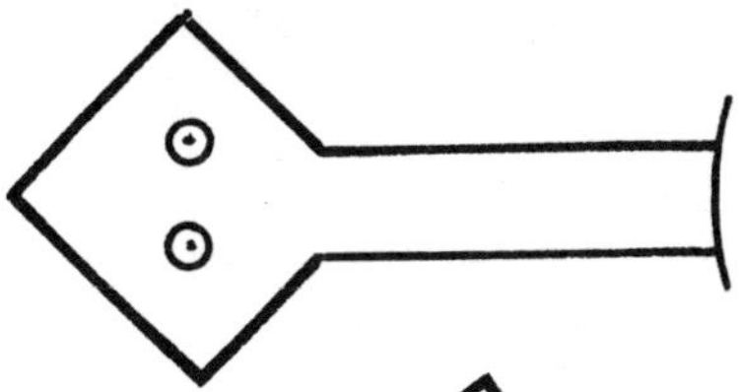

Some of them are on short necks . . . . . .

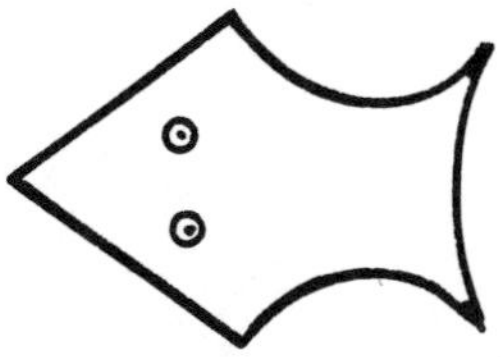

And some have no necks at all . . . .

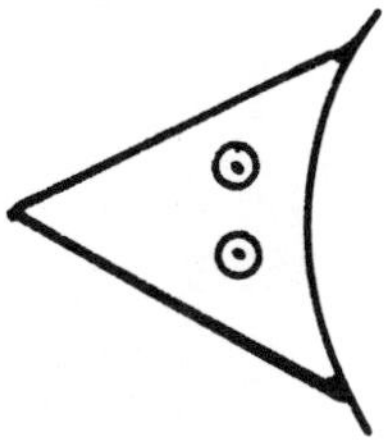

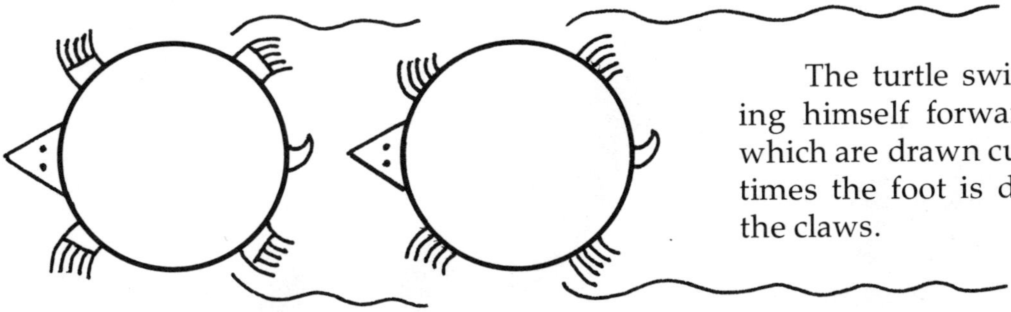

The turtle swims or crawls by pushing himself forward with his short feet which are drawn curved backward. Sometimes the foot is drawn, sometimes only the claws.

The turtle's shell may be checkered . . or cross-banded . . or have squares inside squares . .

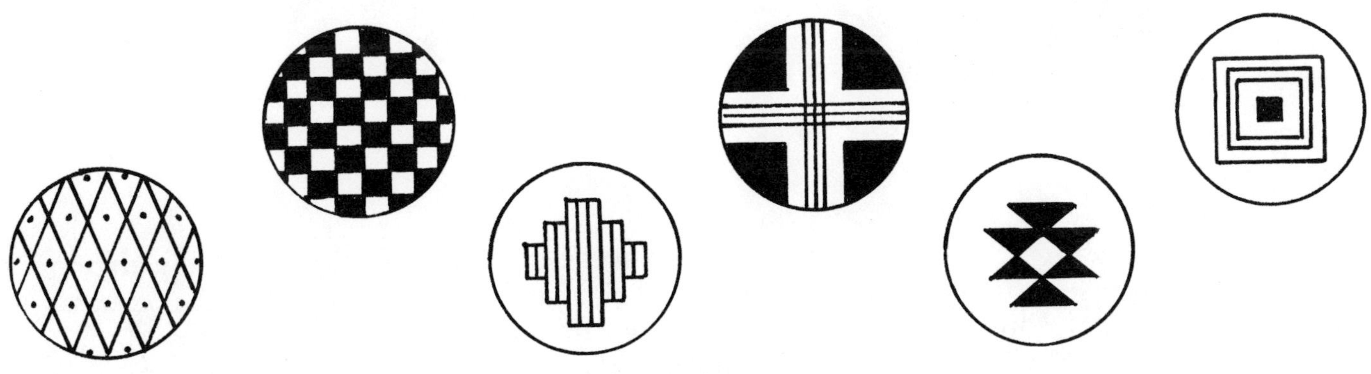

or be diamond-patterned . . or with steps and lines . . or almost anything.

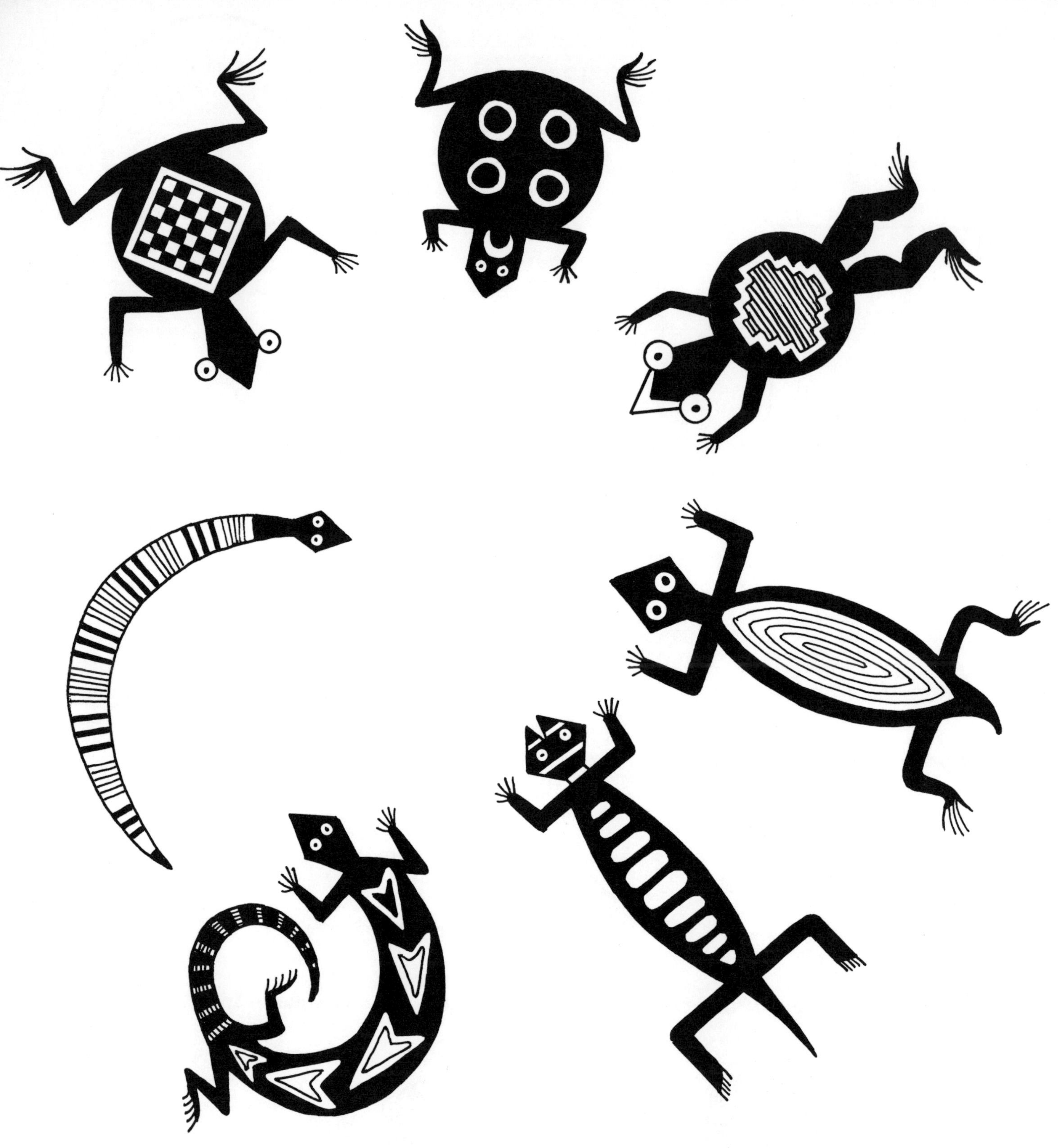

Frogs were equally at home in water or on land, .using their long hind legs for swimming or jumping. Most snakes, too, could swim, but spent much of their time on land, as did the many kinds of lizards that lived in the Valley. All of these creatures can move swiftly, as you know if you have ever tried to catch one.

These may not be animals you would like as pets, but they can be fun to draw. Frogs begin with a circle, adding strong hind legs braced to jump, but no tail at all. You might start with a simple outline like this . . . . . .

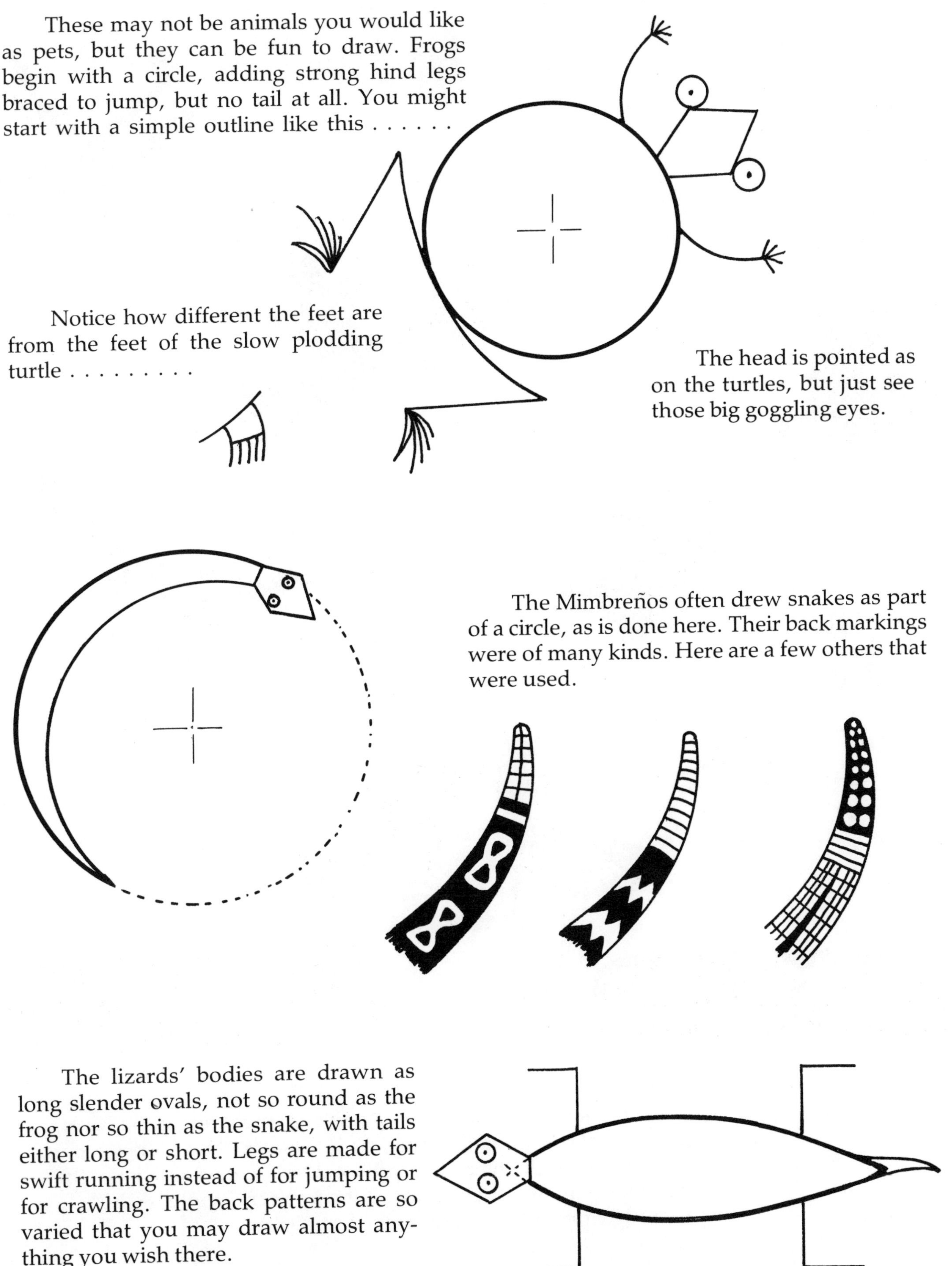

Notice how different the feet are from the feet of the slow plodding turtle . . . .

The head is pointed as on the turtles, but just see those big goggling eyes.

The Mimbreños often drew snakes as part of a circle, as is done here. Their back markings were of many kinds. Here are a few others that were used.

The lizards' bodies are drawn as long slender ovals, not so round as the frog nor so thin as the snake, with tails either long or short. Legs are made for swift running instead of for jumping or for crawling. The back patterns are so varied that you may draw almost anything you wish there.

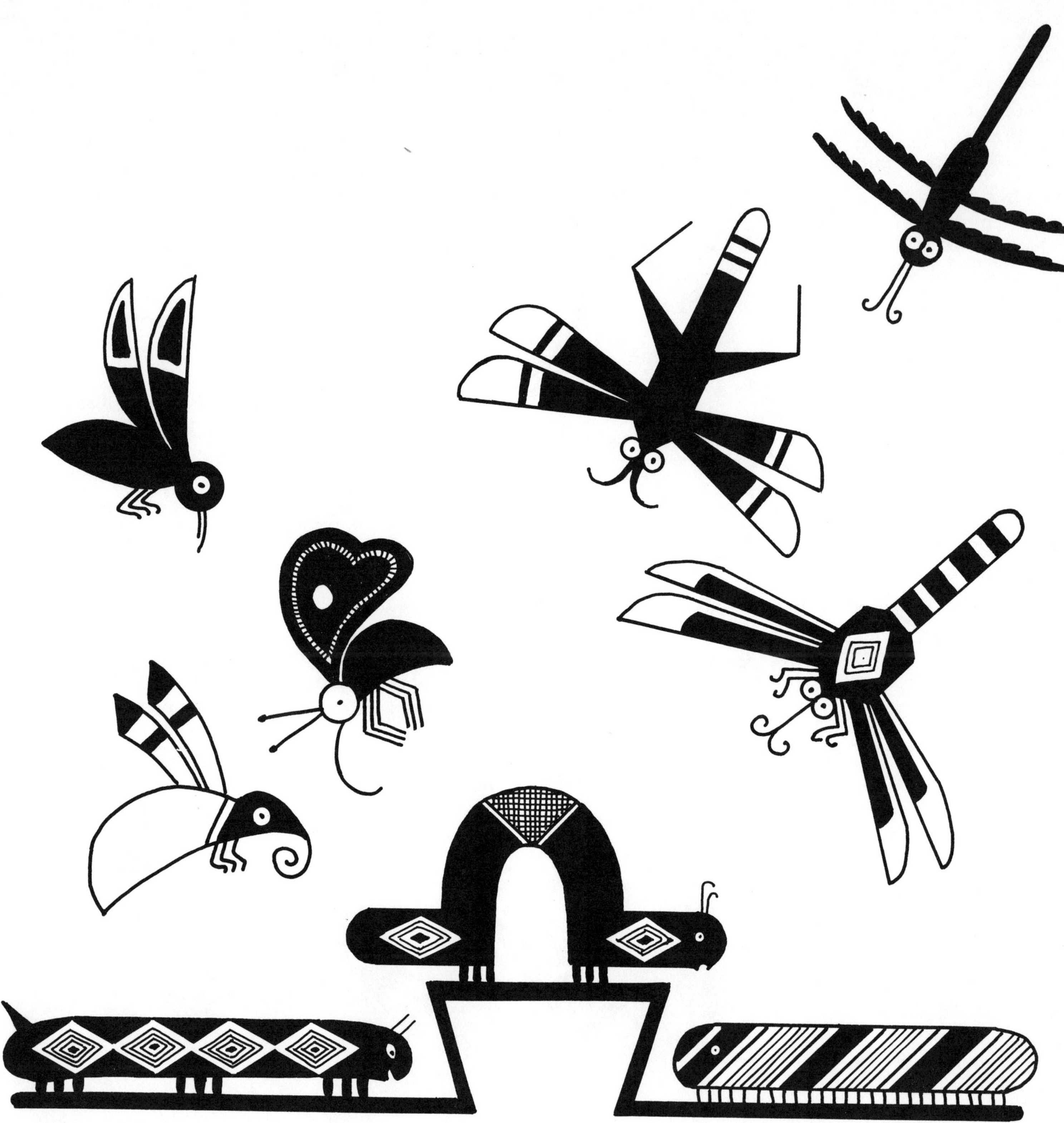

Dragonflies must have been a common sight along the River, as so many bowls were decorated with these graceful four-winged insects. Bees, with their long proboscides, were valued for the honey they gathered. Below are a tomato worm—note his horn; a measuring worm; and a many-legged centipede.

The dragonfly has a thickish body with a thinner long tail. It may have a head or just a pair of eyes and curved antennae. One shown here has two long hind legs, another has four short front legs, while the other shows no legs at all.

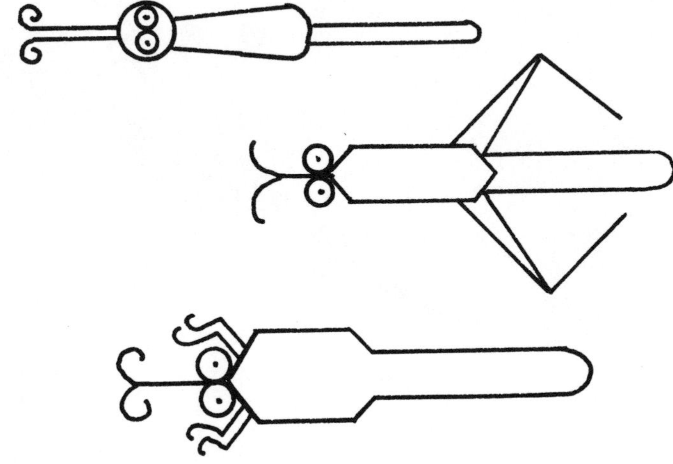

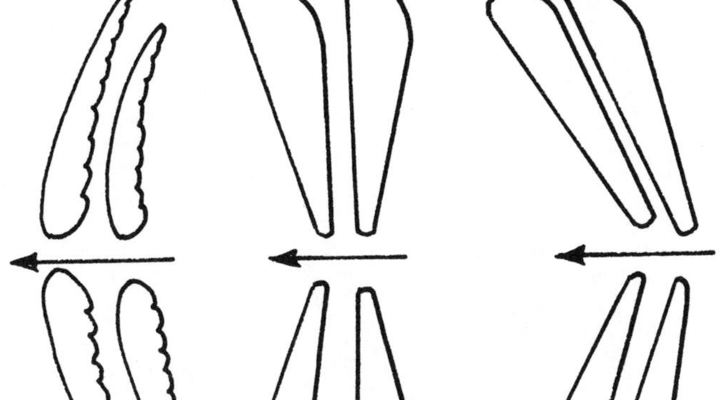

Dragonflies are always shown with four wings, which may be held straight out or slanted back or forward as it flies.

We know these are honey-gatherers, probably bees, because of the long curved proboscides. Each is shaped as part of a circle. Note carefully where each circle center is. Wings are usually drawn as a pair, and sometimes only three of the six legs are shown.

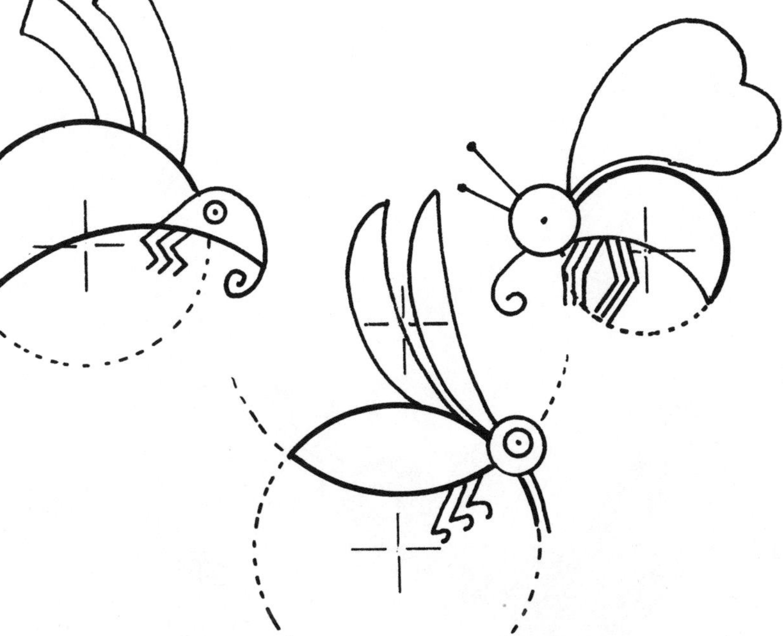

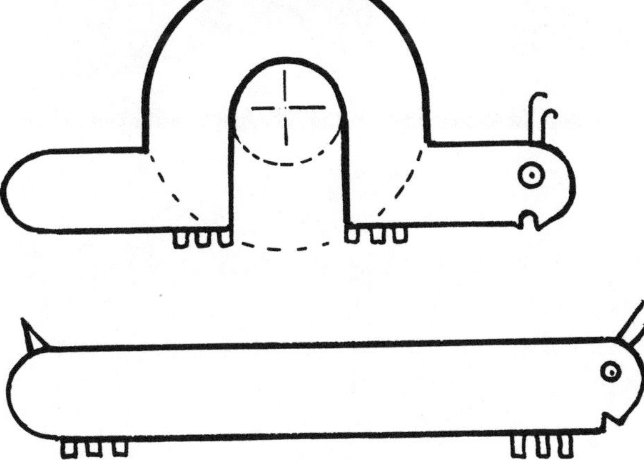

Worms, caterpillars, and centipedes are all shaped like long sausages. If you draw a horn at one end you have a tomato worm, if you draw him humped up on the middle he is a measuring worm, with lots of legs he is a centipede.

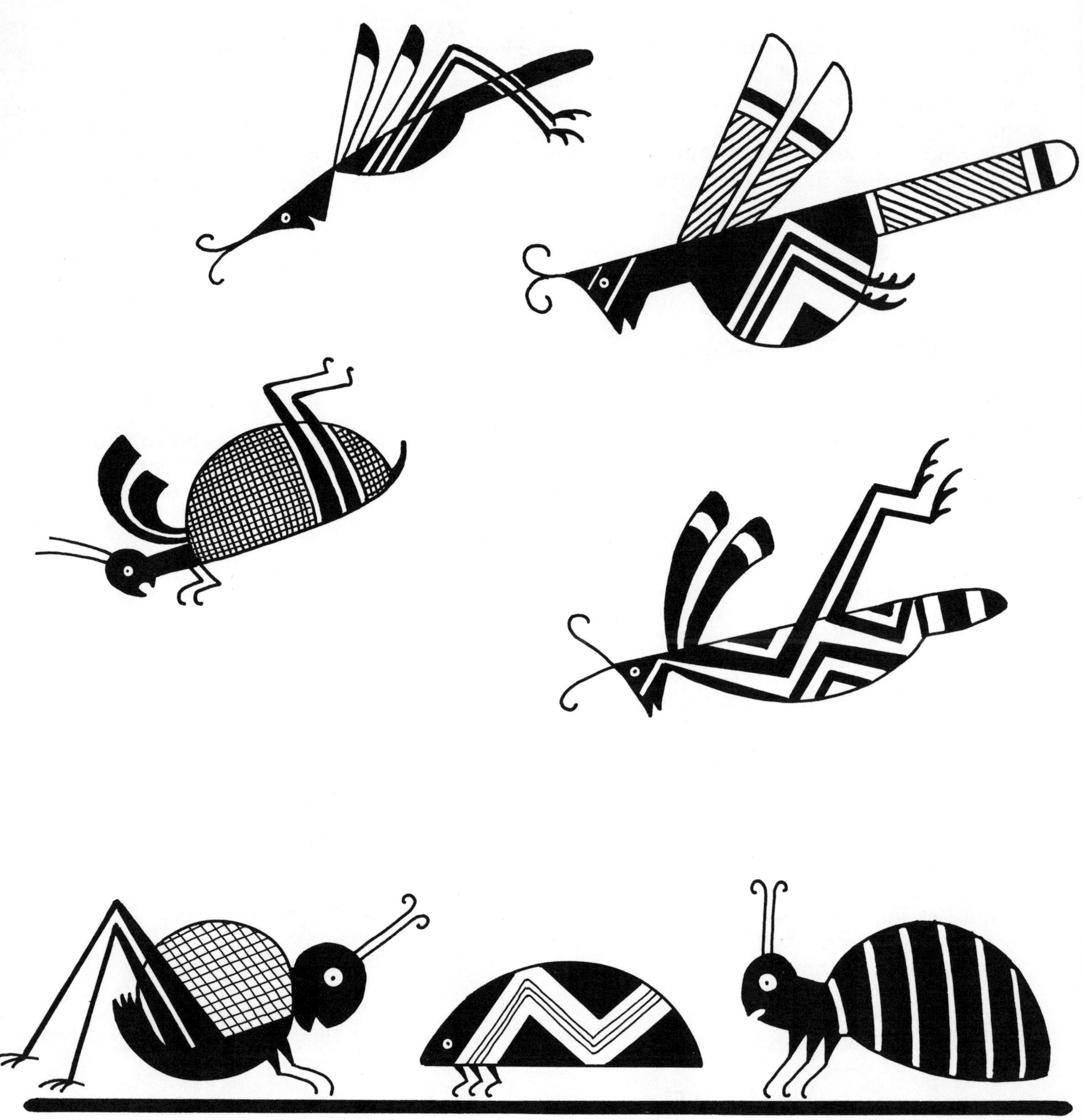

Grasshoppers must have been a great nuisance when they got into the bean fields. Their long legs and sturdy wings would have made them very hard to catch as they flew through the air. Lower on the page are a fat little cricket and two creeping insects.

The grasshopper's body is part of a circle, his tail either short or long, thin or thick.

The head, triangular or round, has a hungry open mouth and two antennae.

Strong hind legs are most important to this insect and may be held high or lower as he leaps. Wings are shown as a pair, either straight or curved.

This little cricket has a circle for a body, and also has long hind legs. Add a smaller circle for the head, with antennae and open mouth.

Here are two bugs we have no names for. Both may be started as parts of circles.

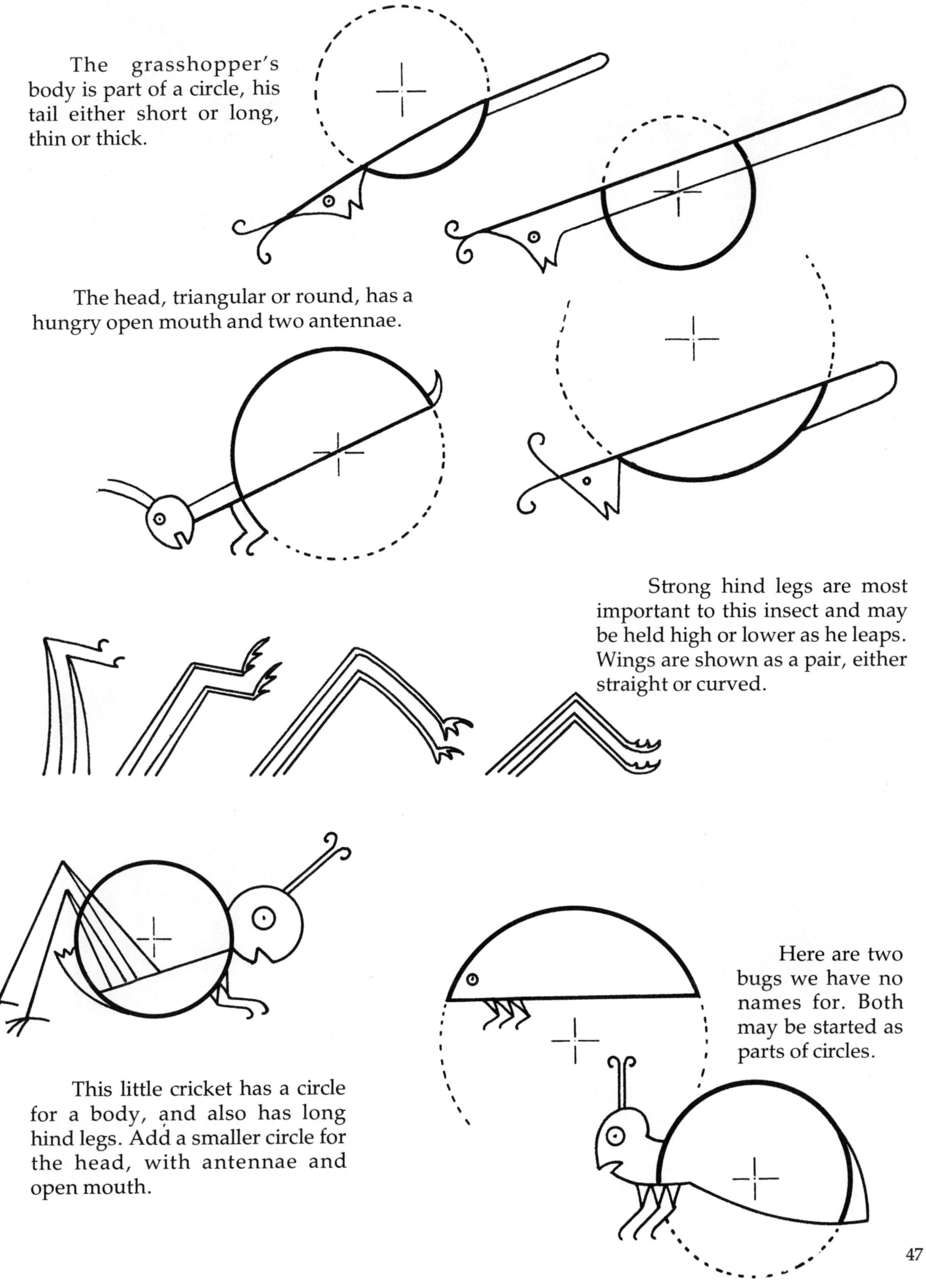

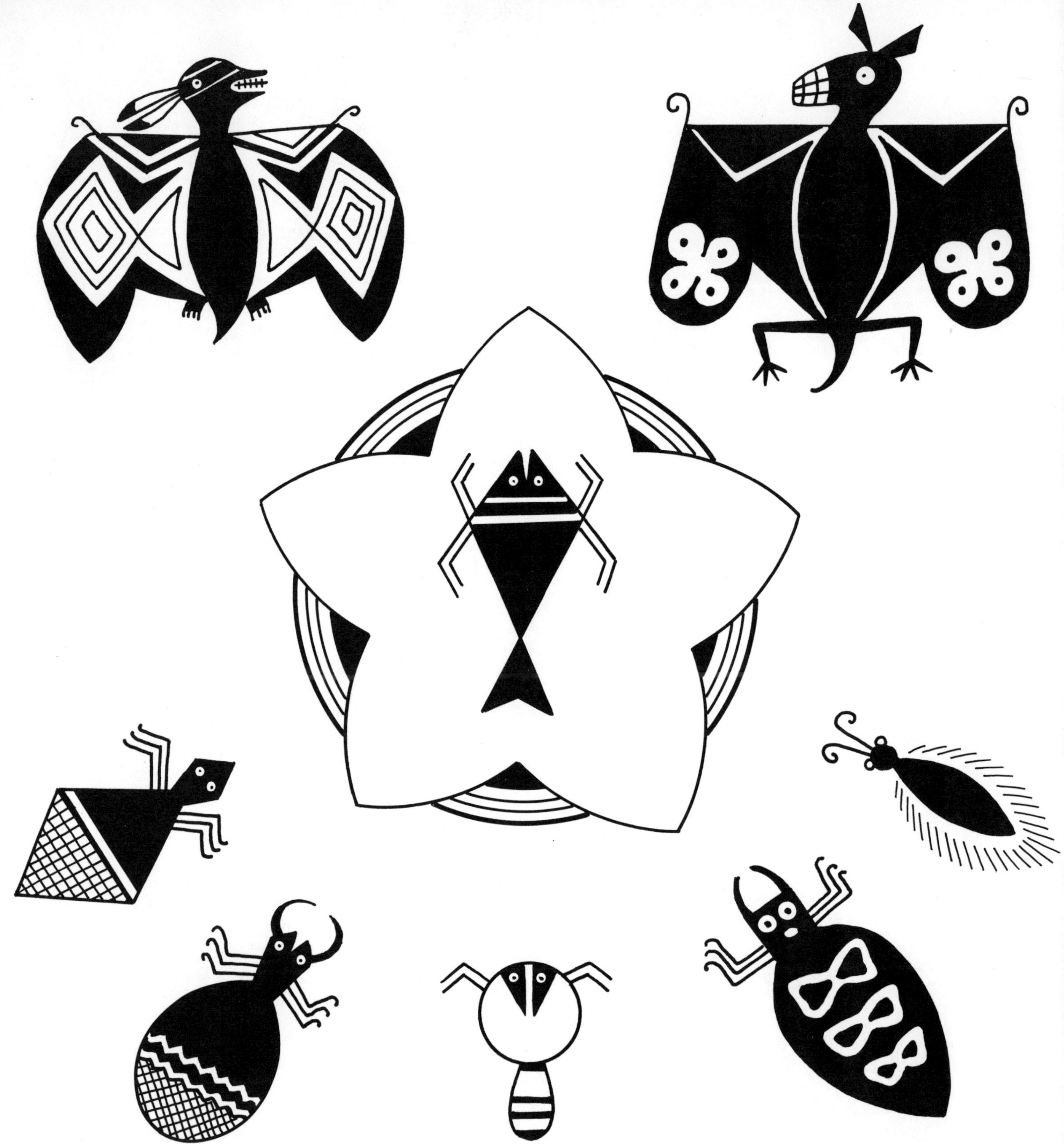

Many bats lived in caves along the cliff sides, coming out at night to feed on insects. Their front legs form part of their wings, spreading or folding them like ribs of an umbrella. The little creature in the center of a flower must be a spider, as he has eight legs. I wonder why the potter gave him a fish tail.

This night-flying creature can easily be recognized by his long front legs with hooked ends that spread his wings. These wide wings often have much decoration, but his small oval body is plain. Hind legs may be small or not shown at all. His head has big ears and plenty of sharp teeth.

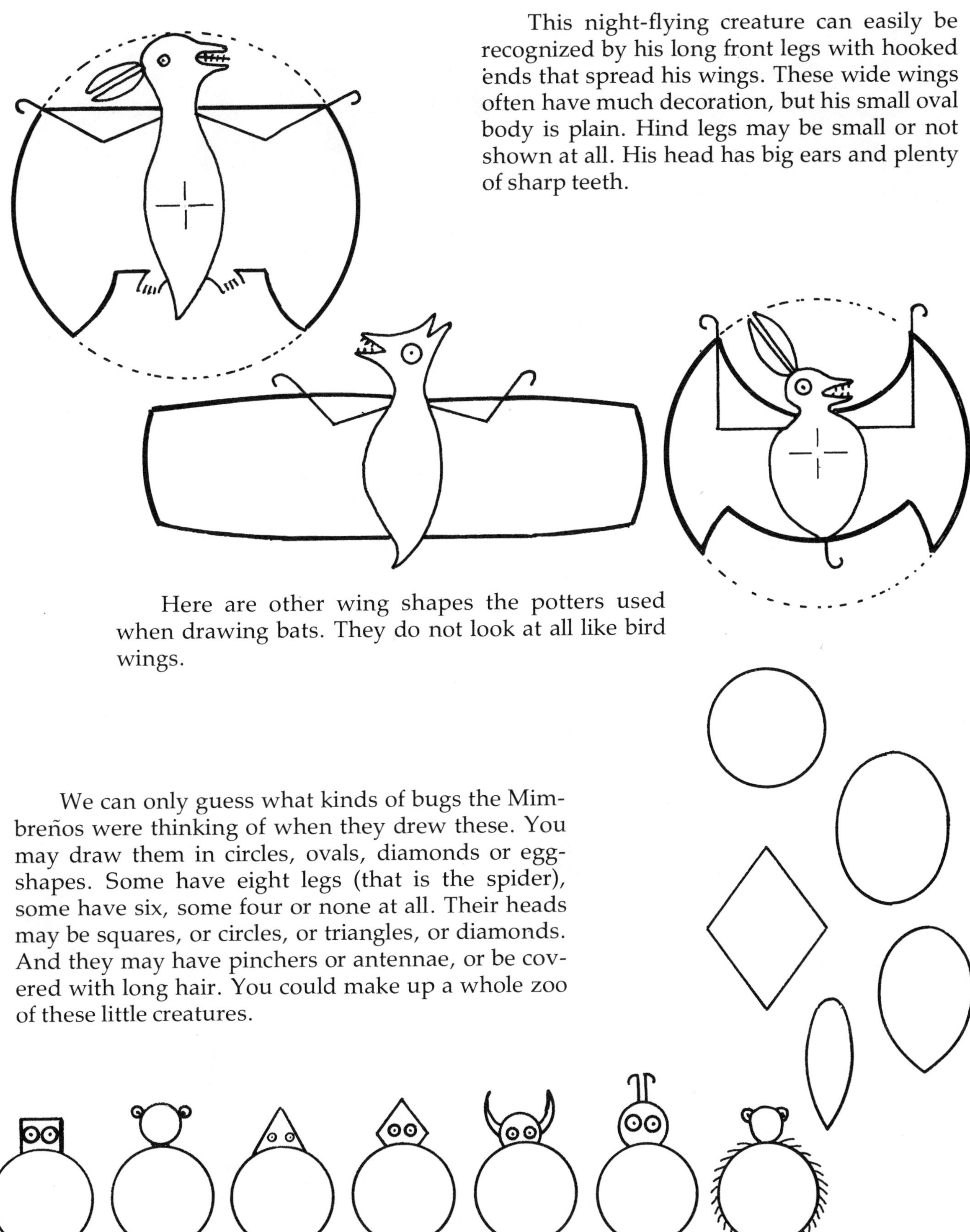

Here are other wing shapes the potters used when drawing bats. They do not look at all like bird wings.

We can only guess what kinds of bugs the Mimbreños were thinking of when they drew these. You may draw them in circles, ovals, diamonds or egg-shapes. Some have eight legs (that is the spider), some have six, some four or none at all. Their heads may be squares, or circles, or triangles, or diamonds. And they may have pinchers or antennae, or be covered with long hair. You could make up a whole zoo of these little creatures.

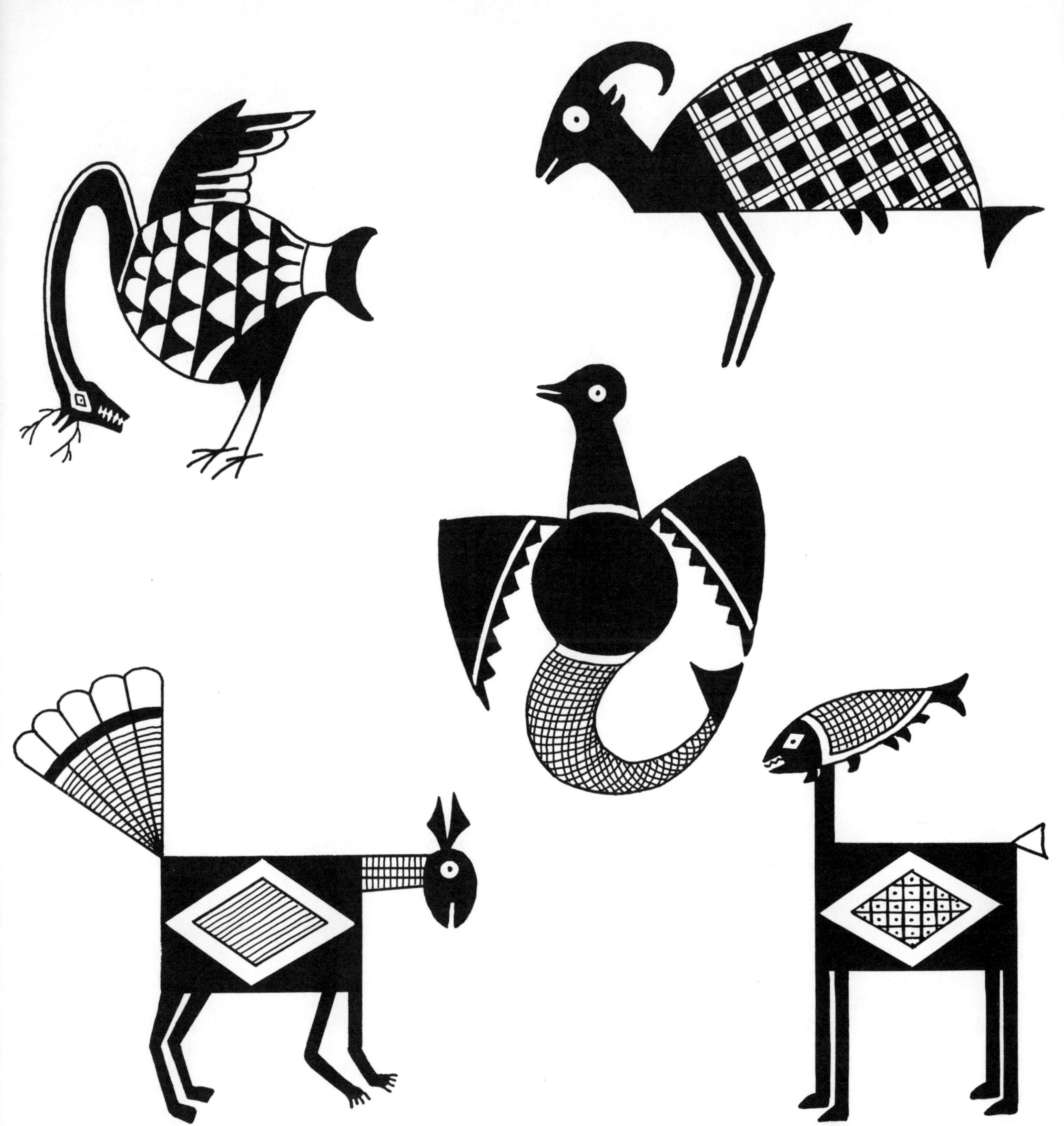

Now, surely, such strange mixed-up creatures as these were never seen in the Valley! Why do you think the potters drew such animals? Experts who have studied them have various theories, but I like to think they were just having fun. Now try drawing your own Animals-that-never-were.

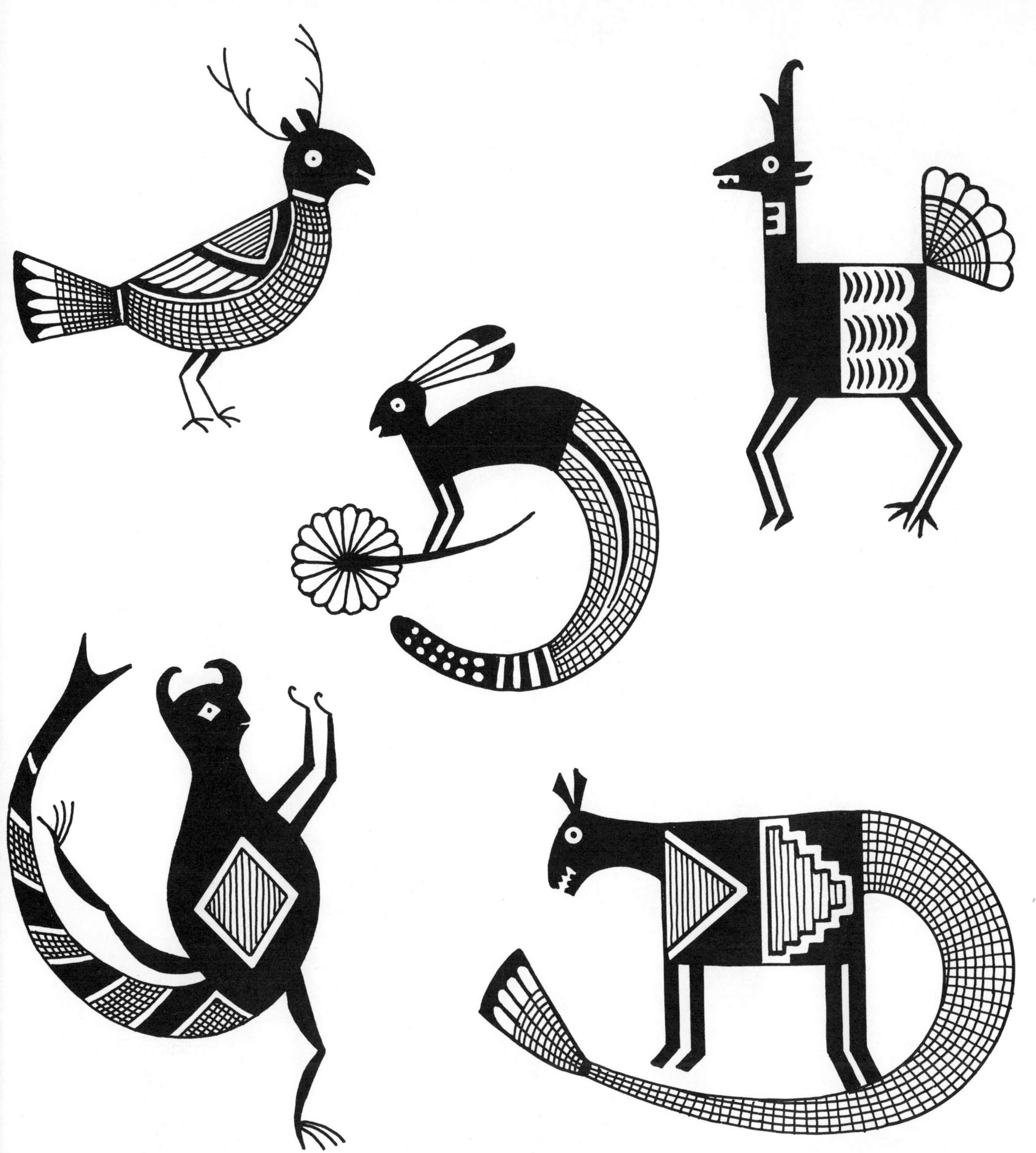

Here is is another page of What-do-you-call-ems. Could that be a "birdeer" and a "turkalope" at the top of the page? Can you find parts of four different animals in that happy dancing creature? You might try naming each of the "mix-ups" you draw.

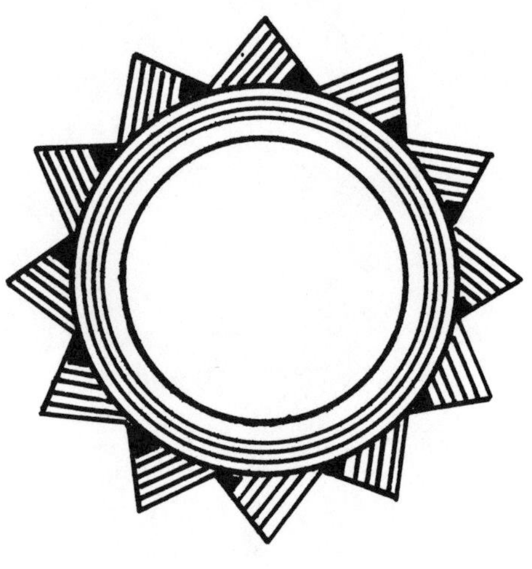

Father Sun was very important to the Mimbreños, so they often pictured him on their bowls or the rocks along the cliffs. These four suns are all circles but with different kinds of rays. The three stars are drawn with four points, as was usual. Below in one corner is lightning in a dark sky; in the other is a turtle carrying a rain cloud on his nose.

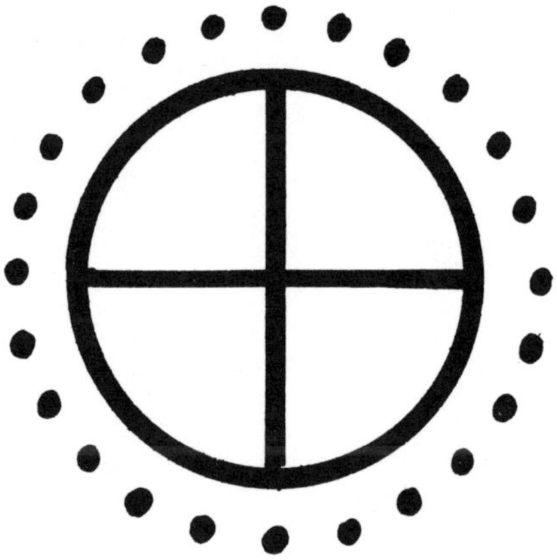

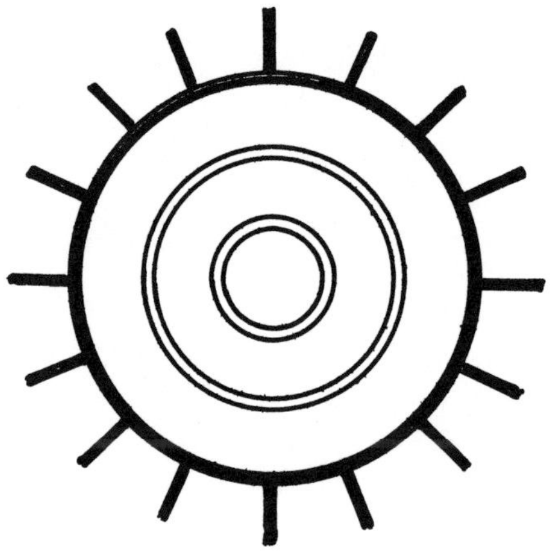

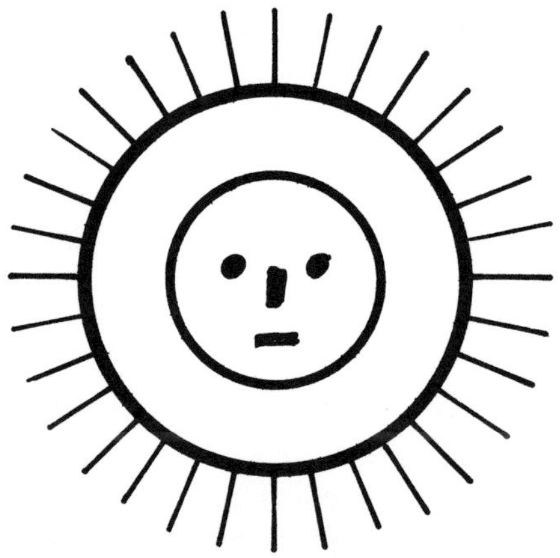

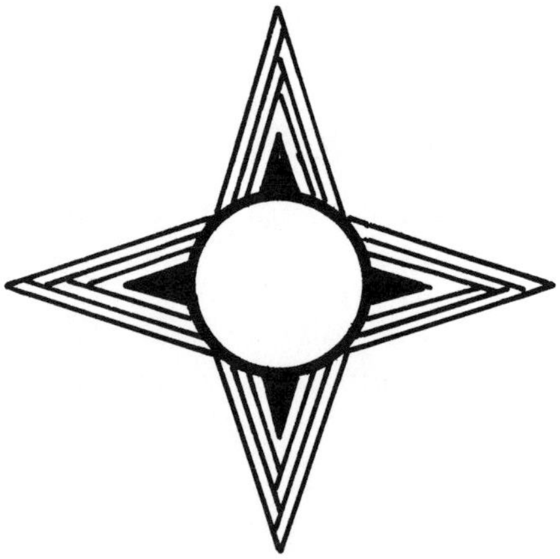

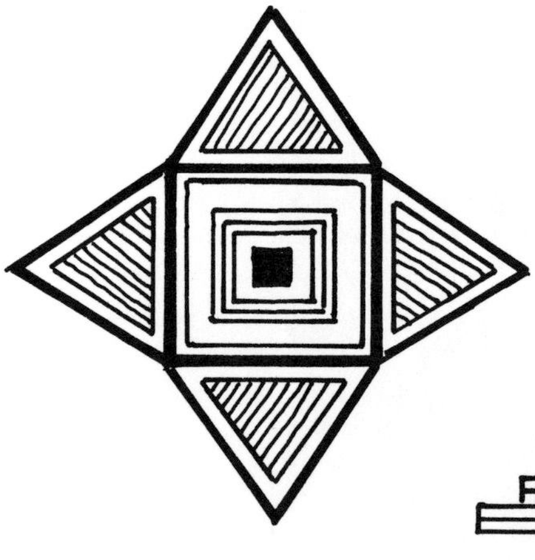

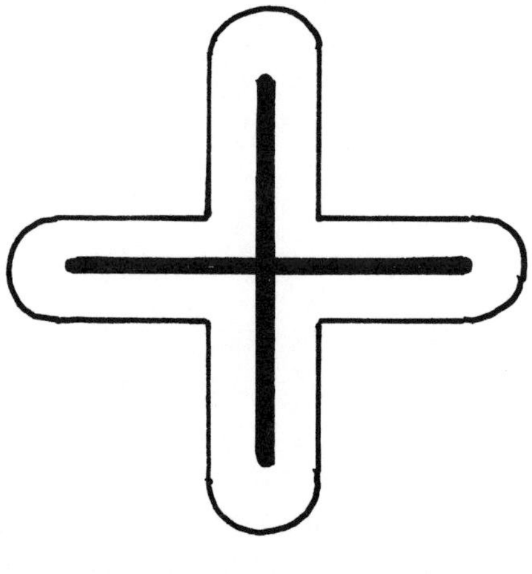

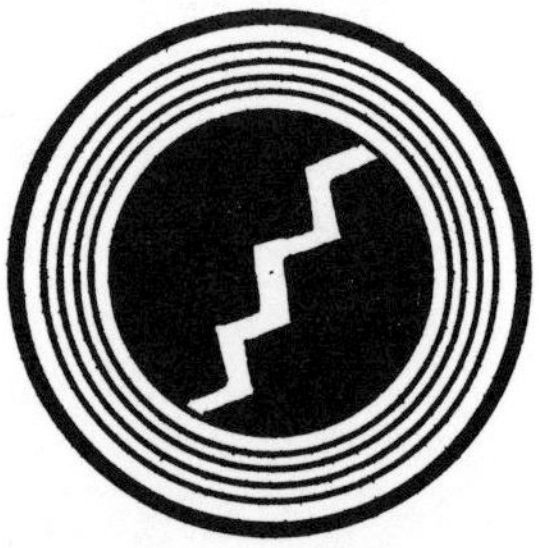

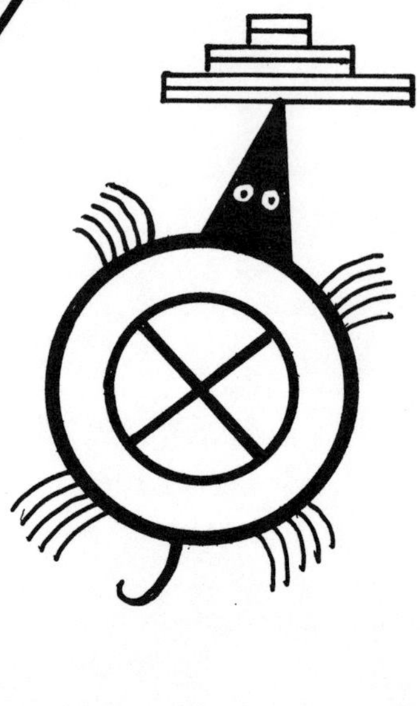

Sometimes the potters of the Valley drew flowers, for these, too, were their Wild Brothers. Draw a circle lightly for the outer edge of your flower, another inside it for a center. Add petals—four or more—round or pointed, plain or decorated.

This is a sunflower, as is the one above it. Wild sunflowers grew thick in the Valley and their seeds were roasted and eaten.

Now would you like to try drawing a Mimbres family? Here is how these remarkable people pictured themselves, —the man with his arrows, the mother with her baby, the boys with their pet bear cub.

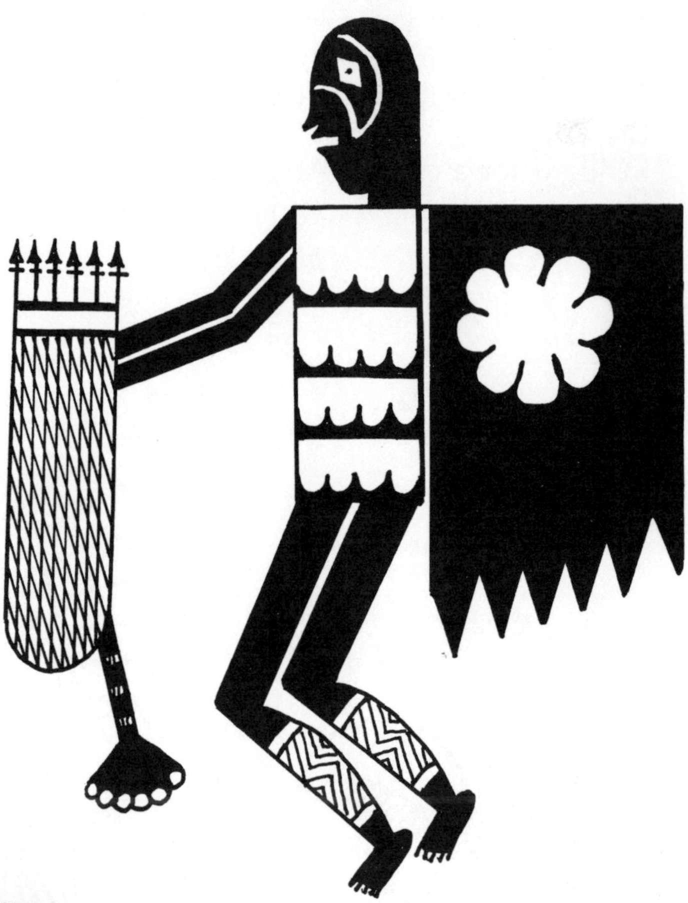

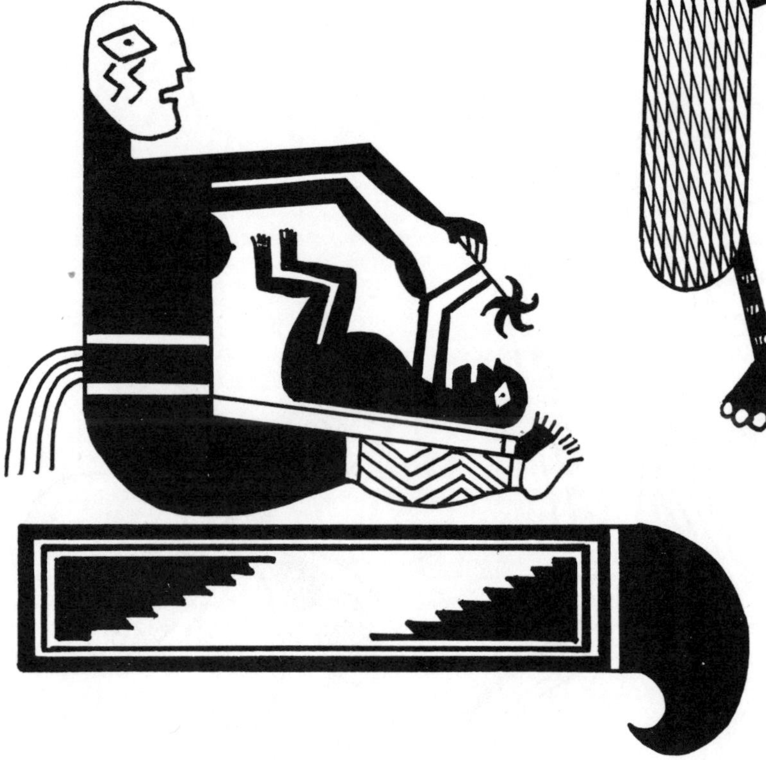

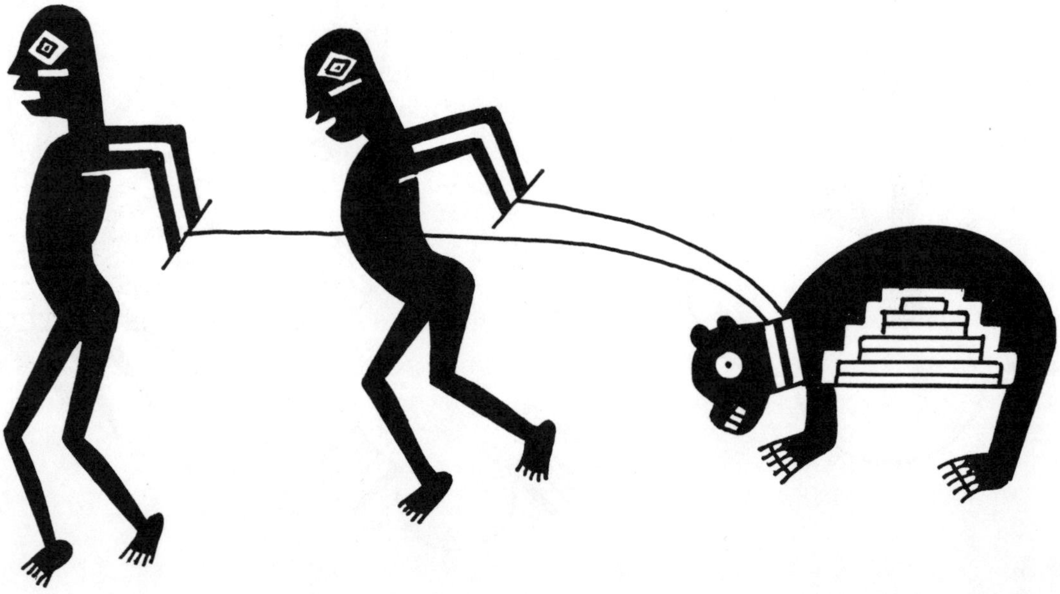

You will notice that all of the family are barefoot, but Father and Mother wear leggings, and all except the baby have face-paint. Father has a fine garment, probably woven of feathers, and a quiver of arrows. The object at his back may be a shield. Mother wears a sash tied at the back, and amuses baby with a whirly-gig. The two boys are more interested in their bear cub than in fancy clothing. You might draw these people doing other things, as gathering berries, building a fire, or trying to catch a frog.

The two Mimbreños below are dressed for some important occasion, perhaps for a dance to pray for rain, or in thanks for a good harvest. Both wear fine headbands, face paint and sashes, and one has a many-stranded necklace.

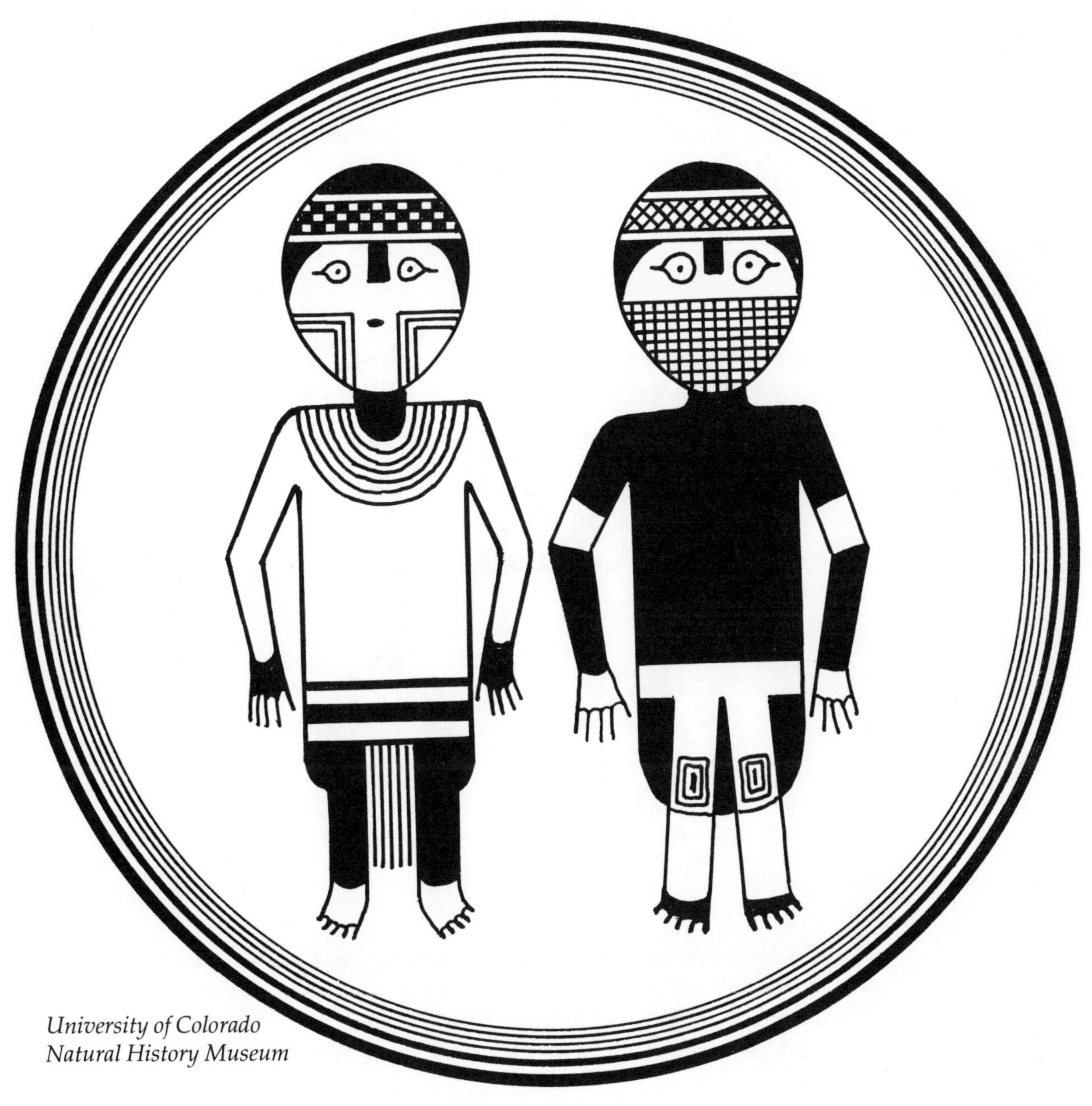

University of Colorado Natural History Museum

Now that you have shared with the Mimbreños their pleasure in drawing the wild brothers they knew so well, you may be wondering what ever became of these talented artists. This is a question that has never been completely answered. Archaeologists say that for some reason they left their homeland probably a century or more before Columbus came to America. Possibly there were a number of very dry years when the River began to fail, and there was not enough rain for their fields or to produce plentiful feed for the animals. Whatever the cause, they moved away, and people on the move have no time to make beautiful painting in bowls. Some think they went far south into Mexico and joined with western tribes there. Others believe they drifted northward, up the Rio Grande valley, and scattered among the Anasazi pueblos of New Mexico and Arizona. The pottery designs of the Zuni and Hopi and other groups may have been influenced by these wanderers from the south. But never again, anywhere, did any people paint animals in quite the way they were painted beside the Mimbres River and in the villages of neighboring valleys about one thousand years ago.

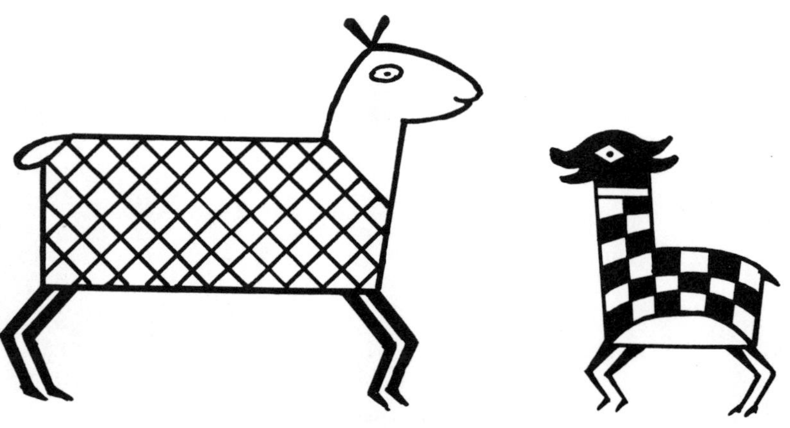

Mimbres ceramic designs represented herein are drawn from examples in Museums and private collections, and from standard archaeological works; Bradfield, 1931; Cosgrove and Cosgrove, 1932; Nesbitt, 1931. Any artifacts other than Mimbres were drawn from photographs of the articles.